OUTBREAK OF PEACE

Satsang with Isaac Shapiro

Isaac Shapiro
Outbreak of Peace

Compiled by Dick Sinnige

Design: Premram
Cover Photo: Martin Jäschke; photo on page 41, 51 and 59: Elsja Lewin

Printed in Germany on chlorine free bleached, recycled paper

ISBN 3-9805879-0-8

To all of those who are serving Love's call
by assisting in organizing Satsangs,
transcribing Satsang tapes, editing, proof reading
and generally making it possible for me and my family
to be on the road and available for Satsang,
many thanks.

Thanks to Dick Sinnige and Premi who made
this book possible.

To my beloved wife, Kali,
for the willingness to live in the fire of Satsang,
inviting me to a vulnerability and nakedness in this play.
You are my own heart.

Sri Bhagavan Ramana Maharshi

To Sri Ramana
– indweller of every heart –
whose spontaneous awakening and steadfast purity in *That*
has served mankind
and continues to draw seekers to the flame of Truth,
pulling us all into the Heart.

Sri H.W. L. Poonja (Papaji)

For Beloved Papaji,
my spiritual Father, Master,
igniter of the Heart,
whose unswerving devotion to Truth, Love, Atman*,
is inviting us all
to an outbreak of Peace.
There are no words that can convey my gratitude.

Atman - lit. "eater of thoughts"; in Vedanta the immortal real Self of human beings, identical with Brahman, but used to refer to Brahman as individuated within the person.
Brahman - ultimate Truth, impersonal Absolute Reality; substratum of all that exists.
Vedanta - system of Hindu thought of non-dualism.

Preface

Outbreak Of Peace is based on the Satsangs of Isaac Shapiro that took place in Amsterdam during 1996. Satsang is a meeting with Truth, which is always here and is usually overlooked. We can watch a bird flying in the sky, but when asked "What do you see?", people say "A bird." The sky itself is overlooked. The bird comes and goes, the sky remains. It may be cloudy or sunny, the sky is always there. In Satsang Isaac points to the emptiness in which everything appears, which is always here.

At the age of nineteen, Isaac had an experience of unconditional love. He realised that his way of life until then, had been a mere shadow. The day after, he resigned from studying medicine and decided that he wanted to be free. He spent many years looking at the functioning of the mind and its relationship to consciousness, and after some time, he wanted to develop a way to communicate his insights.

He started to work with people, showing them how they were using their attention. This work was powerful and quite successful, but for Isaac something was still missing.

Disillusioned with what he had experienced with Gurus and teachers, he was not interested in finding a Master. Then he heard about Poonjaji, also called Papaji, from a friend whom he could see had blossomed in Truth. After seing this beauty, he had to go to see Papaji in India.

Papaji, a Sage who awoke through the grace of his Master, Sri Ramana Maharshi, regarded by many as the living embodiment of the Supreme, left His body September 6th 1997.

His invitation to Truth proved to be what Isaac had been searching for. All his questions were answered – he recognized the Truth of Himself - he was Home!

Then came the moment when Papaji told Isaac "You have found the Diamond. Now go, and be available for Satsang."

In Satsang with Isaac everything can come up and can go, jealousy, anger, fear and love, the fire of hell as well as the light of heaven. Deeper than this you are. In this recognition there is laughter, tears and wondrous silences. Satsang is not about getting anything or getting anywhere. To get you need something and someone to get it. In Satsang one can see that there is no two, there's only one. Deeper than intimacy, higher than the sun.

However wild the storm, however rough the shores of existence, the ocean of Awareness contains it. We are It all the time and It is everywhere. There is no hiding place from the Source of all creation.

Isaac responds to every question being Awareness itself, Truth shining without a shadow of compromise. This love transcends all space and time. Satsang is a hot fire and the diamond is shining.

What a joy it is to have these beautiful dialogues with Isaac. They are natural, and yet completely revolutionary. It's an overflowing of Truth and It is here with us. We are invited to Satsang, a meeting with our own Self. Yes, we are one. Yes, Love is pulling. Such eternal beauty is here. Welcome to this outbreak of Peace. Let It have you!

Dick Sinnige
September, 1997

The poems at the beginning of each chapter are
inspired by Satsang.
These poems are overflowings of Awakening.

These words come from the interface
of Being and non Being.

That place of dissolving
and undissolving,

Reflecting the lingering fragrance
of that ecstatic intertwining

That long breathless kiss.

MIKE FLATT

I

Let there be peace and love amongst all beings of the universe. Om Shanti, Shanti, Shanti. Namaskar*, welcome to Satsang.

Please feel free to ask any questions and speak about any new outbreaks of freedom.

Do you meditate and what do you feel about meditation?

There are so many techniques that people call meditation. Ultimately, when you are doing some activity to get somewhere, even if it is to get silent, you are missing what is already here, because you are trying to get somewhere else. Truth is already here. The only moment you can know Truth is now.

If you are making any effort, this will take you out of now and reinforce the sense of *I*. It will take you somewhere else. It will make a subtle game of different experiences and the evaluation of these experiences. When you are ready to end all of this, you come to Now, to this instant. Don't evaluate or compare. Don't intend anything or try to get anywhere. Truth must be already here. You can have many experiences by doing different techniques, but these experiences won't help you.

When you say, "I'm going to meditate for half an hour," you have already tied your mind outside meditation before you have started because you are actually saying, "After half an hour I am not going to meditate anymore". To be in this instant, is meditation! You are always Here. Simply be with your direct experience of who you are,

Om - According to Hinduism the primordial sound from which all creation springs
Shanti - Peace
Namaskar - Sanskrit greeting: *I greet that in you, which is the same in me.*

which is for 24 hours and is always Now. You cannot be who you are for only half an hour. To be who you are is real meditation. In meditation there is no sense of separation. Like the river, it came from the ocean and when it returns to that, it becomes ocean itself. When the attention comes back to its source, all sense of giving attention to anything disappears together with the sense of a personal "I" and only Beingness remains.

So at that moment Consciousness is face to face with Itself.

Not even face to face with itself. There is only Consciousness.

So meditation is happening in that emptiness. Then whatever I am doing, it doesn't matter. There is emptiness and that which arises in emptiness.

This is true meditation; this is true understanding.

So there's no searching for any objects, any experiences. Because everything is appearing in me and I'm not looking for what is appearing in me. I'm only looking for the discovery of myself. Then maybe there is one moment of luck in my life, in which That reveals Itself.

Every moment is this moment. Even the idea of this moment appearing is just an idea, because this is appearing in Consciousness itself. Consciousness is already here, even when there are thoughts or objects. So to try and hold on to some idea of everything disappearing, makes the idea more important than the Now. Then there is some waiting, some effort to get somewhere, to have something happening. Consciousness is here, you are That.

This feeling of *I* that rises, is natural to this body-mind. This ability to focus is necessary for this body-mind to function. Normally people are attached to this functioning of *I*. They believe it to be themselves. You can see that this has to happen for this body-mind to function. This is not You. It is merely an activity that is arising in something much more subtle, absolutely vast, boundless.

Then there is this willingness to let this *I* function and not to be associated with it. It seems personal, but it's not. It's simply a functioning of this body-mind; it has nothing to do with You. This body you had no choice about; your conditioning you had no choice about. So you are not responsible for the actions and reactions of this personality, which is here by itself.

Do you live constantly in that vision or viewpoint?

I say, look at your direct experience of who you are. Is this a viewpoint or is this direct experience? Now you speak of your direct experience. Who are you? Not some idea in your mind. The concept of constantly comes in your mind and this is an evaluation and a doubt about your own state. If you pick up this doubt, then you're worshipping doubt. See it as only a thought. Stay with your direct experience of who you are.

I understood that enlightenment is something very sudden and very big. Now I feel it's like an understanding that gradually happens.

What we call enlightenment is only an idea. The mind works with standards: good, bad, right, wrong, this is enlightenment, this is not enlightenment. This is the way the mind functions. Remove mind, remove any thought, and what is left? Just **Here Now**! A natural state, an innocent state. No idea, no reference points, no relationships. When someone has some relationship they can call this enlightenment. When you don't have any relationship, you can't call it anything. Anyone that says, "I am enlightened" is lying, because no person or personal state is involved.

Then what's this whole experience of golden lights and flaming skies?

This can happen if you take enough drugs or with certain breathing exercises or if you push on the eyes very hard. (laughter) You don't have to run after any experience! Really, just keep quiet.

There is much misunderstanding about this whole concept.

There are so many ideas. The only moment you can know Truth is now. This instant. You tell me what's Here, in between thoughts?

Being.

What else is needed?

Only practical things to function.

Practical things to function – that happens by itself. Nobody is interested in just Being itself. Everybody is interested in some far out experience. They don't examine what is Here. If you really examine what's Here, something rare and beautiful happens. You start to notice that by being Here, some subtle things are happening. When you are just willing to leave everything, including these subtle experiences, Truth shines!

Every day I prayed to God. It felt good, but the last two weeks it didn't happen. I didn't pray to God. I'm confused about it.

In our society, there's this way of functioning that produces separation. We feel separate from each other, from God. This is called duality or split mind. In this split mind, we don't feel at home. We feel lost, so we pray to God. We ask God for help and when we're praying to God we feel good, because now we are opening ourselves to what we think is divinity. But that continues this activity of asking God for something. It keeps us wanting something. It feels good, but it also keeps us in duality. It is very much part of our conditioning. We are brought up with institutionalized religion.

I was not raised with it.

It was in the culture whether you grew up with it or not. At some point you start to look a little deeper. In this looking you see that whatever manifests, whatever object is there, must come from somewhere. Every object owes its existence to the subject, every object, even the idea of God. Now we come to the subject itself, *That* from which every idea arises. Once there is duality, there is some sense of needing something, or wanting something, or being vulnerable, or being scared.

So we have to come to the subject from where all of this is rising, the whole universe, the idea of God, everything, every experience. This we have to find in this lifetime. Once this is tasted, naturally many habits and activities start to drop away. It can feel uncomfortable when you had some comfort from these activities.

It feels very uncomfortable.

You think, you are being disloyal to this God or this Guru. Then you start to look. What is this? Who is aware of this?

But what do I do with all these questions in my mind? What is this that we call God?

We don't have a word for the Source. This Source from where everything rises. We call it God and because most people don't have the direct experience of this Source, it's objectified and conceptualised and made into some thing.

But now I have nothing. I was happy I had God.

Now enter this nothing and see where God originates from. See the Source of the personalised God. This is God itself. Only through incorrect understanding it is made into something.

Make an experiment and look beyond the mind. Do you see any God? Who do you need to pray to Here? This God that you're speaking of and praying to, is a fabrication of mind.

I have the thought that God is an object so I should stop thinking about God, but then I'm not happy.

Then you're only thinking that you've stopped thinking about God. If you just stop, then what's your experience? Now stop and from Here you speak. Don't move the mind. Just Here. This instant, this micro-second. What's your experience?

A lot of light in my head.

Any unhappiness?

No.

What do you feel in your heart?

Peace.

Peace. So lovely.

What is the purpose of meditation. What is it actually doing? Because I did it a lot and there was much clarity sometimes.

What most people call meditation is concentration. You concentrate either on the breath, a mantra, a certain part of your body or on your Guru's face. There are many different meditations. When you concentrate the mind doesn't move. When the mind doesn't move, there's an experience that is called *Samadhi**. If this becomes very intense and direct, you can experience *Nirvikalpa Samadhi**, in which there are no thoughts for hours or weeks. And if you really focus, you can do it for years.

There was one yogi who was very focused and he could stop his mind. The king heard about this and said, "Someone that can stop his mind for one week, I'll give him the best horse in the kingdom." This yogi was very proud of his accomplishments. He came, he sat quietly and went into Samadhi. One week passed, one month passed, one year passed, ten years passed. Finally he came out of Samadhi. He said, "Where's my horse?" The horse had become very old (laughter).

What we are speaking about here is actually called *Sahaja Samadhi**, which is called the natural state. This means the end of the mind, not just stopping the mind. If you stop the mind, the moment you quit the mind stopping technique, the mind will start again. What we are speaking about here, is *Atman Vichara**, inquiring into the source of the mind. *That* which is aware of the mind, is called *Atman*. This is not an object. When you're used to focusing on an object, you can bring your mind to one object with a lot of willpower and keep it there. And there's some health benefit to that, they proved that in TM*. But it is not the end of the search. For the end of the search, you have to see, who is aware of the searching activity. Who is aware of the mind. The natural state is simply to see who you are and stay with This!

I remember that Nisargadatta also refers to meditation. That he also did it himself.*

He was only looking to see who he was. His Guru told him, "Find out who you are." And that's what he stayed with. This is called *Vichara*, which is inquiry. No matter what comes, you ask, "Who's aware of it?" "I am." Then, "Who am I?" When you're around someone whose mind is quiet, he can point you very quickly to This. You experience Yourself and this is the greatest luck.

Samadhi - Absorption in bliss
Nirvikalpa S. - The *samadhi* in which no differences arise or are perceived
Sahaja S. - Natural absorption in Emptiness while apparently engaged in the world
Vichara - Self-inquiry
Nisargadatta - Indian sage, who lived in Bombay, India (1897-1981)
TM - Transcendental Meditation

Well here I am again Lord.
Trying to write you down.

But how can beauty, so strong,

That it rips away seeing and feeling
in one heart filling instant,

Ever be written down.

Why is it that these words
can never reveal their source.

And must remain the moon.

Only able to reflect the suns glory.

MIKE FLATT

II

This is something very new for me. I don't know what it is.

Yes, don't know!

But I want to know, because otherwise it could disappear again.

Now you don't know and it's here. When you want to know, it disappears. It disappears only when you want to hold it. If you want to know and hold it, then this activity puts your mind in the future. This *Now* is so precious. Right Here! Kiss it. This inner kiss, not to know it, not to understand it, just let it kiss you. You kiss it and you are kissed. When the mind wants to run, you tell it, "I'm completely in love with Now. I would like to spend time with you, but I don't have any, because I'm absolutely in love with Now."

How does this work when I'm in a very busy street, with loud sirens and ambulances with people all around?

Where did the mind go?

The mind ran away.

Now you can see this. It ran somewhere.

So that's what is happening?

That's all. This is just made up. Because this doesn't exist now it is a dream. If you are dreaming and a tiger is chasing you in the dream, how do you get away from the tiger?

I wake up.

You wake up. Like that. So to wake up is very simple - It happens by Itself. This habit of the mind, to run from past to future, is what troubles you. One thing is clear, no matter how much we worry, it doesn't change anything.

So I'd better focus on the unchangeable in such a situation.

Forget even this. Don't focus on anything. No focus. No trying. No you. What's left?

There's nothing.

There's nothing and this is okay?

Yes.

I asked somebody about how to protect myself from the influence of everything else. He told me to build walls. That didn't really make me feel extremely optimistic.

Yes, because even if you build great walls, there are such good tanks and other weapons now (laughter).

How do I accept everything?

Everybody is looking for security. Enough money, enough walls, enough cement, enough something, so that they can feel secure.

This is what's going on, because people feel afraid. Everything that you do to try to control this fear is still playing within the same realm. It doesn't take you out of it. Even now there is Awareness here, Awareness of all activity, all thought, all perceiving, everything. But Awareness Itself, nobody notices or pays attention to. We think of ourselves as somebody, but clearly this body itself is existing in Awareness. There has to be Awareness for this body to even exist.

Outside we see a universe. This universe is perceived through the senses. The senses are perceived by the mind. There has to be awareness of this mind. So now, this Awareness itself, you don't have to do anything for it. You are that Awareness in which the senses, the mind and the universe are appearing. Any understanding you are aware of, so it's prior to understanding. You are aware of the five senses, so it must be prior to sensing. You can't sense Awareness and you can't understand it. You can't get to it. It's already here. Any trying to get to it, you will be aware of this activity. So this Awareness itself, can you speak of it?

It does have some qualities of being not attached.

Even this non-attachment is appearing in Awareness. Even non-attachment is just something that is appearing in it. Awareness itself doesn't have any qualities. See if you can find any quality to this Awareness. Any boundary, any limit, anything lacking? What do you find?

I'm extremely tired.

So now, tiredness comes. This is some sensation appearing in Awareness. When you have been efforting, of course there will be tiredness. Awareness itself requires no effort. It's already Here. You don't have to do anything for This. In fact any effort, any intention, any thought will hide it. So now, for one instant, don't think anything! Speak. What's your experience? Where do you begin and end?

I see images.

These images are objects appearing in Awareness.

They're stones falling down a mountain.

These images are objects appearing in Awareness. You see that they're objects, right? Awareness is still prior to this, prior to any image. I spoke a little earlier about people having to be in love with Truth. This is a story, because it doesn't matter what you come here for. You can come here for any trouble, any garbage and Truth can kiss you. It can happen. However, if you're running after garbage and are persistent about it, then Truth has a hard time kissing you. The moment you put the garbage down, Truth kisses you. It's very attracted to you.

Is it possible to stay in the stillness and put your mind into your work? For me, stillness is very hard to combine with talking to somebody.

So now you're speaking, and this speaking is happening in Awareness itself. It requires some attention to speak. With no speaking, you can bring your attention more to Awareness itself. Some attention is needed for speaking. Clearly you need to function in this world. Just keep your mind still and take care of what needs to be taken care of. When it kisses very strongly, just sit quietly and let it kiss and then carry on with what needs to be done.

For some rare people it starts to kiss so strongly, that they simply cannot do anything anymore. If it starts to happen spontaneously for you, then existence will take care of you. But you can't fake it and you can't make it happen. To a few saints this has happened spontaneously. Standing in the kitchen cooking, and forgetting cooking, forgetting everything. Only God is on their mind. Only this Peace is on their mind. Everything is burning and they're enjoying. But for most people, as soon as the food starts to burn, the nose can't handle the smell (laughter).

"

Could you talk about the future?

Nobody knows the future .

Oh well, there are a lot of ideas concerning the future of the world. Like the climate changes and the wars happening all over the world. I see a lot of awful things happening.

We don't know what is going to happen. Nobody knows. When we try and figure out the mind of God, generally what ends up happening is we feel afraid. We can look at things and they look terrible. But then something happens and we realise that it was just absolutely necessary for the next step. Yes, there are a lot of warning signs. Everything is pointing out that something big is about to happen but we don't know what will happen. We do know, that if our minds are disturbed, what we bring to this moment is fear.

I read and think a lot. I don't give peace to my brain.

This is what happens. People think and think and try to organise life to work out in a way that they think will be good for them. John Lennon sang, "Life is what happens while you're busy making other plans." We make many plans and then life is what happens to us. Life goes the way it goes. It doesn't mean you shouldn't plan. It doesn't mean you shouldn't try to take the best care you can. Your conditioning will continue. Let this continue, but see who you are. Planning will continue, just like breathing continues. This you don't have to trouble yourself with. Now take one moment between birth and death, to see who you are.

I was always a spirit. In the womb of my mother, and before that. I will lose my body someday, but I don't care so much about the body. It's only my soul and my spirit that are eternal.

Now you say "*soul and spirit*". We have heard of soul and spirit, but I'm asking you for the direct experience of it. Not something you've heard or read about.

I am a spark in the universe.

This still means there is some mind. Bring your mind beyond spark even. Who can see the spark? Who can see the universe? This universe is appearing in You. You experience this universe through your five senses. Just check and see. How do you know the universe is here? Through eyes, ears, nose, mouth and touch. This is how we know the universe. From the universe go inward. There is Awareness of this seeing, smelling, tasting, hearing, touching and also thinking. In *This* the whole universe is appearing.

So we have to find *This*. We're going from outside, to This, This in which everything is appearing. So close your eyes and for one instant don't do anything. No effort, because Awareness is already Here. Any doing, any effort, there is Awareness of - beyond any effort, beyond future, beyond past. In this moment, Here, Now, everything is appearing, even the past, even the idea of the future. Everything is appearing Here, Now and we have to arrive Here.

The witnessing of thoughts and feelings is clear to me. But there is also Awareness of the witness itself. Somehow that confuses me.

This witnessing activity is the ability that we have to see a thought, to notice a feeling and to notice what our relationship to these is. It is the ability that we have to move our mind. You can focus on your hand holding a microphone or move your focus to the weight of yourself on the chair. You can move the mind like this. There is Awareness of this movement of mind. Not only the ability to focus on these different things, but also to notice this movement. So what is it that notices these movements?

It is noticed in a sort of quietness.

In the quietness this noticing appears. People use words like Consciousness or Awareness for this. This that notices, is there any sense of personality with it, is it personal?

No.

This is your own experience, not something that you've read in a book. We are ordinary people looking together. What we are talking about is natural. Once you look, you can see for yourself. You don't have to be a yogi and you don't need any religious belief to experience this, just the willingness to see for yourself.

And that's enough?

That's enough. This space in which any movement can be seen is Here already. You don't have to do anything for it. It's Here already.

And it is everywhere.

You are *That*! Most people are convinced that they are *I*. Every night in Satsang we look for the *I* and nobody has found it yet.

Today I struggled with this and when I came back to Silence it was gone.

Yes, that's the beauty.

There was the ecstasy of God.

But when looked for
There was no one there to be burning.

A Flame without a candle

MIKE FLATT

III

Why does no effort feel like I am making an effort?

It doesn't feel like an effort, it just feels unusual. For example all your life, your head was tilted and somebody does some bodywork on you and gets your head straight, it feels that you are leaning over. You just have to get used to it.

"

When I am happy I never ask, I just accept things. It is because of suffering that I am trying to find a way out. Why does the mind do this? First it gives me trouble and then it wants to be free of it.

You are describing why it is so rare that people ever come out of their mind, because we value the mind as a problem solving device. First the mind is making a problem for us. Then we use this very mind, to try to come out of the problem.

When I take distance, when I see it fighting, I see it is trying to liberate itself.

That's why you come to Satsang, because here your mind stops for some time. It gets quiet and you feel peace. You feel happiness, love and at Home and recognise that this is so beautiful. Therefore you come here.

But my mind wants this peace too.

The mind thinks, "I want to come out of this trouble." It keeps thinking that it can solve this trouble. This is why it is so tricky. Again and again it keeps on picking up the search. It is very rare for someone to really end this story of the mind. Just by grace you'll find a Sage who has done this. It is very rare, but you need just one instant to taste the value of it, one instant to taste no trouble, no mind. Then you know, "This is all I ever wanted." This is beauty, this is love, this is the end of the search.

I tasted that very strong, because I never focused strongly on the mind.

So now you start to see that there is actually nothing you can do about it. You can't do anything about the mind. If you try and think about the trouble, it doesn't bring you anywhere.

I can just step out of it.

You can step out of it. This stepping out of it just happens by itself. It happens, not from me or you doing anything. It happens by Grace, because it is not a doing. It is actually the absence of doing. Therefore it is invaluable when nobody is doing anything. That's why we don't do anything here. I advise you not to meditate, not to do anything. Then you make yourself available to Grace and Grace can kiss you. Like sleep, when you want sleep to kiss you, to take you in its arms, you have to give yourself to sleep, otherwise it can't take you. If you stand up on one leg and stick your arm out and try to sleep, it won't work (laughter).

Same thing here. You don't have to meditate or make any effort. Just simply be Here, that is enough. You don't have to understand. For the first time, you don't need to do anything, then something will kiss you and you know this kiss and enjoy it very much. If you are struggling and you keep struggling, then it won't work. Even if struggling is happening, just let the struggling be there. Don't fight the struggling. Don't do anything!

I bought a walkman and I am listening to Satsang all day long. That's a way of doing.

That's not a doing. That's a love affair. No problem. What do you find?

Beautiful things.

This Beauty draws attention to Itself. It is a love affair. The Sages say that you must have a love affair with Truth for it to work. You have to be in love with Truth, with beauty, then beauty will be in love with you. If you are in love with worrying and trouble, then worrying and trouble will be in love with you.

I have been listening to Satsang for a couple of days and it all seems so passive to me. Being a Yank, I know about many books and a great deal of techniques. I've gone from one to the other. Then you always have to do something and now there's nothing to do. I feel something is missing. I don't want anything for nothing. It seems so passive.

So even this *it seems so passive* means that there's not passivity. Because *it seems so passive* means that there's still some evaluation. You are very welcome to evaluate, after you've tasted this experience fully. As long as there's evaluation, you haven't tasted what I'm speaking about. You have to put all evaluation aside for a moment. Now, in this instant, **Now**. No evaluation. What's here?

The point.

The point, yes. Now you can evaluate. Now evaluate this point.

I've been understanding that you're not supposed to evaluate it.

Now evaluate it even. Watch this process of evaluation.

Is this necessary or are you just giving me something to do? (laughter)

It doesn't matter. Once you see who you are, you can do what you like. What do you like?

I like to fight for this freedom and now it's coming so easily.

So, look at all the energy you have.

It's true. There's lots of energy left over. It just feels like the step between Being and discovering.

This Being is a constant discovery. Right at this Point, you just sit here and watch it. Just see how rich this Point is. All the subtleties of the universe reveal themselves in your own Heart.

It's daunting how simple it all is.

It is. My own experience was that I really wanted to find freedom, so badly that I was willing to risk my life, anything, to find it. And then I met Papaji who gave me the final piece of the jigsaw-puzzle. It was right under my nose, something I'd never thought of. It just had never occurred to me. That's all and that was it. Once you've tasted this Point, you can see that all searching is useless. Then you'll find the mind will recreate reasons for searching. As you get involved with it, you start to feel the crunch. It comes in your mind again, "Oh, I don't need to seek. So what is this activity?" Then this activity becomes crystal clear.

You see it for what it is. It's just the mind spinning on itself. It starts to reveal itself and as you see it, it falls away. Then other layers of this conditioning, of this cultural bias, that we all grew up in start to reveal themselves, just by itself. Without doing anything, just by simply being who you are, everyone you meet is touched. When someone speaks to you about something that they are going through, you know it from your own experience, not from some book you've read. You can meet them in this as themself, as your own Self. When Papaji told me, "Go and be available for Satsang," he never told me what to do, not once.

Just like you haven't told us what to do.

He never gave me a message to give to people or how to do it, or what to do, or anything. He just said, "You found the Diamond, now go!" It's a fire, because the tendency of mind to think that you know something comes up. I could see people trying to be a teacher and misleading people, even though they did not realise it yet. I could see that possibility for myself. It scared me, because I realised how tricky the mind can be.

So I kept my head at Papaji's feet, because I knew that He is like the sun. Any garbage that came up, as long as I stayed around Him, would be seen. Ultimately, once you've seen, you don't need anyone. If you want to pour gasoline on this fire, then you come to Satsang. Simply by being here, the focus is on That. All these people are focused on That. So the fire gets very hot and mechanisms of mind are revealed very fast. But in your own process, in your own time, it will reveal anyway. So Satsang is not necessary once you have seen yourself. It's just for those people who really want to burn fast. You stay around, but it's not necessary. It's a natural process that will happen by itself.

You said that the mindless state is the natural state. Now I'm asking myself why it is so difficult to find this natural state.

Before you ask the question why is it so difficult, first check to see if it is difficult, because everyone that experiences this natural state says it's very easy.

This I experience now, but not always. So it does not seem so natural.

Let's talk now about your actual experience in this instant. Everything else will be past or future. Here Now, just Here quietly, not doing anything, not having to get anywhere, just Here, this moment, very fresh, not past, not future, do not let the mind run. The mind wants to say "It was difficult yesterday, it will be difficult tomorrow." We know this story. But nobody likes to stay Here. So let's see, what is your actual experience? Just Here, just in this instant Here, you speak. What is your experience?

There is no question anymore.

There's no question, so simple. Is this being natural difficult?

No!

When people get an emotion or sensation that bothers them, I hear you tell them not to identify with it, not to try to change it or get rid of it, and to be quiet and see what happens. If you do this with everything that bothers you, is that the solution?

People find themselves in trouble, they feel afraid, not happy with their life, and they want to come out of this suffering. Some people are very serious. This man here in front used to be very serious (laughter) but his face is relaxing and he doesn't know why. We have these habits and don't know why it is like this. We wake up in the morning, and the mind is troubled and at some point, we want to come out of it, therefore we come to Satsang. We go to some place where we think we can find peace. Normally we find some teacher and they put more intellectual knowledge, which is garbage on our head. To come out of the trouble, means you have to see what it is. You can see something that looks like a snake. You turn the lights on and see it's only a rope. You didn't have to do anything. Now there is no snake, there never was a snake. Do you follow?

We think that what we want will make us happy. This wanting produces fear, anxiety and arrogance. Our experience is that we want something. When we get it, we feel happy for a moment, and this never gets examined. We keep wanting things, wanting things to be different, wanting things to be the way we think they should be. This activity continues for a lifetime and in never recognized. When one comes to this moment one gets what he wants, there's peace because there's no wanting. Now you see, this wanting is actually to not want.

Whenever there is upset, you can see that there is some wanting going on. If there is jealousy, there's some wanting. If there is seriousness, there's some wanting going on. People become very serious seekers. They want peace, do you follow? Wanting peace means, in this moment they are not peaceful. Examine yourself and see if there's wanting going on in this moment. Are you wanting something? Be honest with yourself. Remove want, remove any hope, because hope is usually what ties us to the wanting. You hope it will turn out someway that you think it should be. Remove wanting and remove hope, and see what your experience is. Try for an instant and see if you can stay serious, or if you can stay suffering.

I understand. I feel it when I am here. But when you say not to try to change it, not to try to get rid of it, then what about these groups and therapists, trying to help people to get rid of their patterns and change their behaviour?

None of them work. They don't work.

That's what I was wondering. Is it useful to join a group, when you have problems with something that you can't get rid of? Or is it better to stay quiet and just look at it and let it disappear?

Even if it troubles you for many years it will disappear by itself. Because what keeps it alive is the attention you give to it. If you don't give attention to it, what happens?

Then it is not there.

It doesn't even exist. The trick is to get your attention somewhere, where it is so beautiful that it does not want to run after anything else. The habit of the mind is to run, all the time. You have to find something that's more attractive to the mind, because if it's not more attractive then mind will still wander. You have to find some place inside your own Heart that's very beautiful, very quiet.

Once you find this place, and have tasted it for a moment, the mind automatically will keep being drawn back *Here*. It might taste the trouble again, "Ah, it doesn't taste so good anymore," and It will come back. Like this, after some time, all these things will drop away by themselves. You don't have to do anything. But you have to find this place inside your own Heart, that's more attractive.

That saves me a lot of time, energy and money.

Money, time and energy - same thing.

"

Last night I was having these really vivid dreams, as if I was another person. It was strange. My mind reacted to it in the morning. It said, "My God. I was another body, another person."

Satsang is working. You come to Satsang, it's enough. You don't have to do anything, just being here is enough. Like when you get on an airplane, the responsibility is on the pilot, you don't have to do anything. Now you are here and you keep on struggling and fighting, moaning and complaining, but without realising it, things are dropping away. That's my own experience. All of a sudden you look and say, "Wow! Something that would have completely freaked me out happens and it doesn't even touch me. There are bigger gaps between my thoughts and without realising it, this process deepens." You just keep your mind on Truth, that's enough. The real step comes by itself; you don't have to do anything. Your work is finished now.

I have a question about life and death.

I have to correct you already, because it's not life and death, it's birth and death. Birth and death happen in Life.

You have been talking about conditioning. I was riding my bike to this place and I was almost hit by a car. I was wondering why do we try to keep alive?

Every lifeform tries to stay alive and perpetuate itself. This is the nature of every lifeform. It's part of the wiring of the body.

So it's not something that is put on our head, but it's Life itself?

It's Life itself.

I Am
Loves sacrificial lamb.
Thrust into the fire
That love alone may shine.
Burn me lord.
Love explodes and flares,
Crackling and burning.
Let me stand naked.
Let me burn.
Let me die.
Burn me Lord.

MIKE FLATT

IV

W*hen something from outside comes to me, I feel* I.

Something from outside means the senses. We speak about the senses as this feeling of *I*, this feeling of the input of the senses and our relationship to our perceptions, this gathering of information that is necessary for the survival of this body. These senses are needed to be able to perceive what is happening around us so that a lion won't eat us. This feeling of *I* is necessary for the body to function. We say, "I see, think, breathe". Find out, who is breathing. This you cannot find. Breathing is happening, seeing is happening. Is there an *I* that is seeing? Who is the *I* that is seeing?

It's the same as the senses.

It is a sense. So this feeling of *I* seems like it is sensing and thinking. What's your own sense of *I*?

The one that listens to you.

The one that listens. The ears are hearing. Then the sounds go inside somewhere. Now, who is the one that is listening?

Someone here in my chest.

Someone here in your chest is listening. When you ask people to point at themselves they always point here (points to his heart). They don't say, "Here I am" (points to his forehead). So now, this feeling in the heart, go to the center of this feeling itself.

The rhythm of my heart, I disappear in this rhythm.

You disappear in this rhythm. Even the *I* disappears.

But then when somebody hits me, I have to come back to the I.

This thought comes in the mind, "And then I have to come back." This thought is *I* again.

It is as if the I *cannot be gone. It is dangerous to be gone.*

So let the *I* be there. Is the *I* who you are?

No.

It is just the mechanism, so let this *I* function. It functions very well. It is not who you are.

Am I my doing?

When you look now, who is listening? Ears are listening. Are the ears you?

No, the ears are not me.

So, who is listening? Listening is happening. Listening is appearing in me. I'm aware of listening. Now, what is this *I*? Breathing is happening. I don't know who is breathing. Breathing is breathing itself. Seeing is happening. Seeing is seeing itself. Seeing is seeing.

Speaking is speaking.

We say, "I am thinking." But the thoughts just came in your mind. Life is going on and some response happens to life and you say you responded, but the response has happened by itself. This interaction is happening by itself. And you don't know why you are here and I don't know why I'm here. Somehow we meet and somehow I say, "Who are you?" And you respond, "Who am I?" And all of a sudden you see there is nobody here.

You say, there is nobody here. But who is saying that?

It is happening – life is happening. We don't have the language for speaking Truth. Therefore we say, *I and you.* Look, here is this hand and the fingers are wiggling now. I can say these fingers are wiggling or I can say I'm doing this . I see this is my hand. This isn't me, this is my hand. These are all just ways of speaking. So I say *I and you* to point at something.

You're not this body. When this body is laying down dead, we say, "There lays his body," not, "There he lays." There lays his body, he left. What is this that is breathing this body? What is it? Is it something personal? Our sense of ourselves is of being personal. We think of a personal *I*, then we start to look into it and we see that there is awareness of a memory. The memories are personal to this body-mindstream, but I'm not that. Sure, I can identify with that and say, "Yes, this is me." There is an ability to do that. When that ability is exercised and believed in, it causes suffering.

I don't get this.

This thought is there, "I don't get it." These are only words and for whatever reason, the words are not making sense. No problem. That happens sometimes. Actually, when Papaji spoke to me, I had to buy the tape afterwards to hear what he said to me, because when he spoke my mind was completely quiet. I didn't hear anything. I sat there and I said, "Thank you." My mind didn't function, so I didn't understand anything. It doesn't matter. I understand if you don't understand. It's not about getting something or understanding something that we are speaking about here.

•••

Last winter in India, I visited the Shiva temple. The day after whilst riding a moped and chanting to Shiva, I had an accident. The next day I was laying on the bed. The man with whom I lived in the house gave me a Ramana book. When I saw his picture and read about his life, I cried for hours. The night after, I woke up in the middle of the night and I had the most blissful experience of my life. It felt like it was going on for hours. I had these rushes of energy going over my body. And when I opened my eyes, Shiva was in the room. He was asking me to come.

I tell you this, don't go with Shiva! (laughter)

That's what I wanted to ask.

Shiva was very attracted to you when you met Ramana, so you keep quiet. You see who you are, then Shiva will come to you for Satsang.

But that really confuses me.

Being confused is not Satsang. You have to keep quiet. Don't be confused, because otherwise Shiva will not be attracted to you and he won't come to your Satsang. The Gods will come to Satsang, to someone who is simply recognising that from which the Gods appear. Don't get caught in the Godly realms or any other realm. The room where the Gods live is another trap. You have to find from where the Gods, the universe, time, everything is appearing. This is the invitation here.

Every God owes his existence to you. You are first person. God, anything, any object is second person. Anything you see, anything you perceive is an object. No matter how beautiful, it will come and go. You have to find from where it is coming and going. Do you follow?

It seems so arrogant that Ramana and I come from the same Source.

It's arrogance to think that you are separate from that Source. This is split mind. This is not Truth. When you say that the *I* comes from that Source, you've got to see who this *I* is. Find this *I am*-ness, find what it is. You speak *I am* and you say you have this trouble and that trouble. Always any trouble that you have, you say "I have the trouble". So you can try and deal with all the trouble or you can find *I*.

Once you cut the root of the *I*-thought, then you cut the root to every trouble. Find That which is never born and never dies. The body is born and it's dead already. For example take an electric wire. Would you say that an electric wire is alive or dead? When there is electricity in it, we say it's a live wire. With no electricity, we say it's a dead wire. Wire is just wire. Something inside it makes it alive or dead. It is the same thing with the body. Body is only body; something inside makes it alive. When it's gone it's a dead body. Nobody can say what this life is, no doctor, no philosopher. This activity of *I* is arrogance. What is it? It is thinking. Clearly you are here in between thoughts. What's here in between two thoughts?

Nothing.

Nothing. So we have thinking and we have this ability to think about thinking. This is what we have as human beings, we can think a thought and say, this is a good thought, this is a bad thought. This thinking about thinking is what we call witnessing, the ability to see our own thought processes. We feel this as *I*. This ability to give name and form to everything, "This thought I like, this I don't like," is going on constantly. It's giving us an advantage to be capable of dealing with our environment in a more efficient way than other life forms. Because of this we rule the animals. Basically this body is an animal body, and this ability to have intellect allows us to make guns and build cities and drive the animals away.

For a certain period of time it has been working, but we've come to the point where it's not working so well. Because it worked for a while, we really value this thinking and this intellect. We worship it. You're told, "Think, think!" This thinking produces subject and object, you and it, a sense of separation and suffering. All thinking compounds this. Your thinking about Shiva, just makes this sense of separation worse. Everything you do, everything you think, compounds this whole process.

When we suffer, we don't see the cause of suffering. We try harder and it just gets worse. Find That which cannot be gained and cannot be lost. Abandon hope, abandon any desire, and find what's Here already. This is not a casual affair. This is the ultimate Truth of everything. THAT to which the gods, everything, owe their existence. And you are THAT. You've just been mistakenly thinking that you were your thinking process and this body.

So I can simply be?

In our society there's so much pressure to be somebody, that mothers have a hard time to just say, "I am a mother," because to be a mother, you're not somebody special. So silly. Everybody has this pressure on their head to be somebody or to do something or to create meaning. To just Be isn't appreciated. A bird doesn't have this trouble on its head. It's just flying and eating and carrying on its life. So whatever you find yourself doing, that's what you're doing. Whether it's cleaning shoes or toilets, it doesn't matter. It's just what's happening. The trouble comes when we think there is somebody that is doing something.

Isaac Shapiro, Amsterdam 1997

**You cannot go quiet
anymore
This love roars
louder than pain
and suffering.**

**Infinite tears
cry for you
such love which
opens all worlds
which never were.**

YUTI

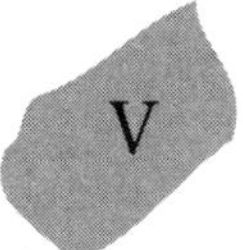

I have a question about anger. You said that it comes and goes and just has to come up. In some religions they say you have to transform negative thoughts into a positive way of thinking. How does that go together?

It doesn't. This path is really a non-path, because it is instant. It is simply to see who you are. To be able to see who you are, there has to be the ability to make a distinction between what comes and goes and what's always Here. Clearly many different experiences come and go. **You** remain. Many different sensations come and go. Anger comes and goes. **You** remain! If you focus on the anger, this means you're giving your attention to something that's really fleeting. Now, bring your attention to its Source, to Awareness itself, or to the space in which the anger is appearing, whichever way you want to speak of it. Just keep quiet Here, and tell me what happens in your heart. In one instant, no time involved. What happens?

Freedom.

So when any thought wants to enter, you can see it wanting to enter. Let it come and go, you don't have to run after it. All your life you've been running after the tricks of the mind. Now keep quiet, and explore this quietness. Kiss It. It's an inner kiss, in your own heart.

If all things, bad or good, are coming from the Essence, then exis-

tence itself is also bad and good. I'm struggling with this.

One way to speak of this is like when we dream. When the dream is not pleasant we call it a nightmare and when the nightmare is intense, it wakes us up. When we wake up, we see this is just a dream. We say, "It was only a dream." In waking state we are receiving information from our senses, and we're interpreting this all according to our conditioning. So each person has their own version of what's going on. This is called a waking dream. When this is bad enough, when this is a nightmare, then you will wake up. If it's pleasant, people usually stay asleep.

I sometimes think that the beautiful things are a dream too.

Yes, everything is a dream. Behind the dream is You – That in which the dream appears. You can understand this with the mind, but This has to be a direct experience. For one instant, we have to put aside this mechanism of interpreting everything, our filter-system. So for one instant Here, you don't do anything, don't put any name on anything, don't try and relate it, or compare it, or understand it, or get anywhere. For one instant just stop, not categorising, no relationship with the mind. This has to be direct experience, then you know for yourself.

You say that we can give our attention to something.

Attention is all that you have.

But still attention does not really like to rest in itself.

In India when a cow has the habit of going to the neighbours fields, even if you beat them, they still go there. The only way you can stop them from going, is to give them better food at home;

then they like to stay at home. When the attention comes home to its own Source, there's a very lovely thing that happens in the body. Very lovely. Therefore, when the mind moves from It, you experience discomfort. Normally we don't notice this movement. We are just used to it and we're used to not feeling very good. Therefore you need to have a taste. Once you've tasted it, then this yearning to stay at Home becomes very strong. You don't want to go anywhere else.

It feels like I've come Home and then it feels as if I loose it.

The mind wants to wander and you notice that all this wandering doesn't bring you this beauty that's at Home. So you come Home again, maybe only for another instant. Then again the mind will run here and there. But by itself, eventually the mind doesn't want to go anywhere. It just wants to stay at Home.

So there's nothing more that I could do?

There's nothing *you* can do. All doing takes you away from home, because it makes it seen as if there is a you.

It's unusual, because to not do, goes against the whole thrust of our conditioning, but this Beauty starts to pull you. You've been coming to every Satsang; I don't think you've missed any. It's like this, you can't resist it.

It's continuous. I cannot forget it anymore.

It starts to pull stronger and stronger.

Is attention not already beyond the mind, because it can observe the intellect moving?

There has to be attention on the intellect for it to move.

Ah, then it starts moving.

So now, beyond all of this. You don't have to understand anything . It's lovely to have a full understanding but to know yourself you don't need any understanding.

I was trying to understand it all.

For a little while, be willing to not understand anything, just don't understand. Don't even try to listen or understand, because understanding can be a big trap. Go beyond understanding.

But isn't it also very easy?

This is understanding again. This is your habit to want to understand everything.

Actually, a lot of times it drives me completely cuckoo.

That's clear, nothing wrong with this. You've developed your intellect very well. It's been your interest. Now go beyond it. Be willing to not understand anything. Now just leave it. Any time you notice the mind wanting to understand, leave it.

I always hear that time doesn't exist, yet when I watch myself or I hear the people speak, we all seem to go through a process that is kind of ripening in time. We are changing and we all have the same immediate bliss experience. The garbage comes up and we fall back. So it seems to me that time is very real.

Seen from the *I*, time is real. The joke about it is, that when you sit quiet you start to notice that there are gaps in this time. There are little moments when there's no time. Usually we just jump over them; we don't want to be in them. We want to stay with what is familiar. In these little gaps, there's nothing there, everything disappears. These gaps are very subtle. The tendency is to identify with this *I*-process. The more willingness there is to stay in the Gap, the more this *I*-process starts to fade out.

Once you see it is a play, then it's called Nirvana - heaven, and you enjoy. When you don't see what it is, it's called Samsara, suffering. Then it seems terrible, because it feels as if there's no way out. You feel stuck in it. You don't see these little gaps. Actually everything is appearing in these gaps, this whole play of *I* , of time and space, of everything, and we take it very seriously, "I want this, I want that. It will make my life better if it happens like this." This is all our arrogance.

To stay Here in the space between, is such beauty. To let life live itself from Here is rare because normally we pick up what we call our life in simple things, like going to get a cup of tea or making a phone call. We go to sleep in our habits of attention. We try to entertain ourselves, or to please ourselves, and we forget THIS.

...

When I'm in This, it becomes almost impossible even to speak. I'm trying now to force myself to speak, to see if I can be in It while speaking.

Stand up now and stay with This. In this Gap, stand up. This is still Here, right? That's why Ramana was drunk. He didn't move from This. He just stayed with This. It's rare that someone just stays with This. Ramana's head was always shaking. People would ask him, "Why is your head shaking like this?" He is from India, they live in huts there. He said, "A hut is never the same after an elephant has been inside." (laughter)

It's just amazing. How can you describe? It's like every cell is being loved by the whole universe. Who can speak it? It's just absolute love, absolute beauty. The mind is quiet. Nothing is needed. So beautiful. Even the breath doesn't move. The yogis knew this connection between breath and a still mind. The breath gets so fine, so quiet when the mind is still, so they were trying to control the breath to have this happen. That's what *Pranayama* is about. But it happens naturally and spontaneously, when you just rest in your Self, and the deeper it kisses, the more you see that there is no end to this beauty.

This morning I woke up with a very stiff neck. I thought, "Okay, let me experiment. Just sit down and be quiet. Do nothing." My experience was that it didn't hurt anymore. I realise that you could do this with everything. Just sit down and be quiet. A lot of people would call this denial.

It doesn't matter what people call it. Denial is actually something else. Denial means something is happening to you and you are trying to get rid of it, so much that you pretend that it's not existing. This is denial. What you are speaking about is that you are more interested in the quietness. That is not denying anything. You are just interested in something else. Before, you were interested in the trouble and now you are interested in the quietness.

What is the meaning of Being?

No meaning. What is the meaning of meaning? Meaning is what you make up. Everybody makes up their own meaning.

But I cannot be here all the time. I have to go elsewhere, like I have to ride on my bike.

You are always Here. Wherever you are, Here you are.

Isn't it useless being here?

Where else do you want to be? Where else can you be?

Because there is so much suffering in the world.

Where? Not Here! Where is the suffering?

But for instance, if a friend comes to me and tells me all his problems.

You laugh! (laughter)

So I say, "I...

How can you speak when you are laughing? Your mother didn't tell you these things?

No. I'll think about it.

I was with a woman for 5 years and about 5 months ago we split up. Still I have a lot of pain. I cry almost everyday for an hour.

So now we come to this instant. Here, your mind doesn't move. If your mind doesn't move to the future, or to the past, what happens in this instant?

No trouble.

This is the secret. When you are crying, it means that your mind is going to some memory. Something in the past and projecting it into the future.

When I look at what you suggest, it works perfectly, of course. But still this crying happens every day. I cannot do anything about it.

Then you have to be very honest with yourself and start to watch to see what is actually happening when you say you cannot help it. There is a certain story that you tell yourself. Your mind goes to it and you go willingly with it. Somehow you value this experience and hold on to it. There is nothing wrong with that. The question is whether you want to be free. If you enjoy the richness of the sadness and the story, then of course hold on to it. If you are willing to be free, don't waste any time.

Do you advise me to stay away from marriage?

Not at all. Marriage is coming together and making an agreement that you're partners, and that you're going to consult each other about decisions. You're living life together for companionship, for the purpose of raising children, for sex. When it's mature, when both are interested in Truth, you recognise that your partner will be a terminal for your drama and you're going to be a terminal for her drama. It's not personal. If you're really willing to be honest with each other and to be more interested in Truth than holding on to any ideas of relationship, this will serve you well to wake up.

Isaac, sometimes during Satsang I cry when people start laughing. It happens when I am touched and I feel relieved.

Sometimes when you come Home you cry, other times you laugh, either one. Tears are streaming, but they are not unhappy tears. Something is touched, and this is beauty. You don't need to trouble yourself.

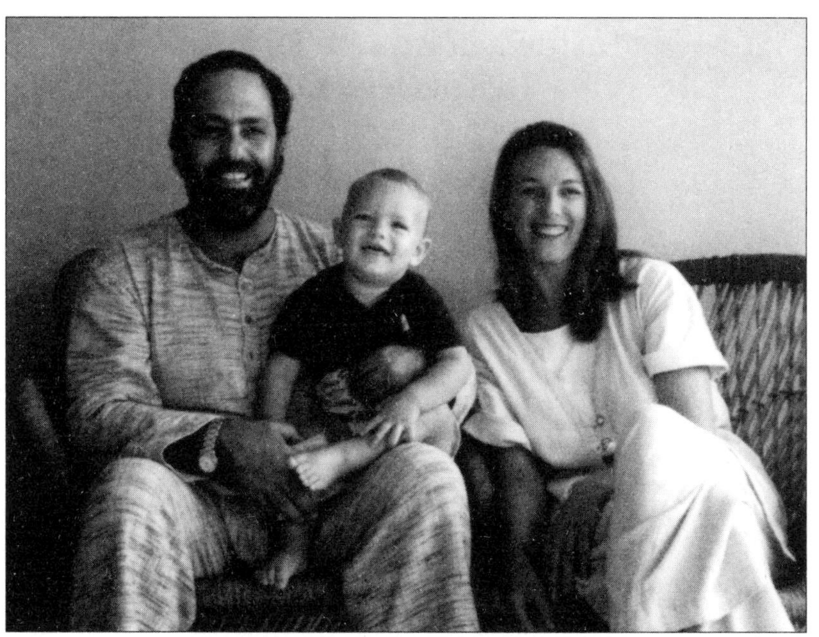

Isaac, Kali and Arun. Lucknow 1997

Inside a complete lack of
experience,
Is a presence.
That's you.

Yuti

few days ago I was very jealous and I tried to stay with it but then I went into what you would call drama. There was no more peace in my heart.

This jealousy was of someone? There are many kinds of jealousy.

My friend was looking at a nice woman. My whole body was shaking and I was feeling a lot of fear.

Then you started to judge it.

But also in the drama I tried to stay with the feelings.

What you're speaking of, is that you're not identified with the drama anymore because even in the midst of the drama there's some recognition that this is a drama.

I know that with my head, but the energy is so strong that the addiction to the drama overtakes me.

Even this means that you see it. Let it be strong.

I see it totally, but I go into it.

Yes, no trouble. Go into it.

But it's not nice, also not for my boyfriend.

How do you know? You have to check (laughter). Some people like it, because they like passion. Many times after jealousy, there are some great things that happen (laughter).

But it's difficult to know how to deal with that feeling.

You have to be honest with yourself. At the moment it seems like your happiness is related to someone. Your whole orientation is around it. Freedom isn't first in your mind. First is your marriage. So when this comes up for you, you are not so interested in Truth, you are more interested in how this affects your marriage, if this jealousy will make your mate go away and if he'll find you ugly in this. So you judge yourself. The fact is that he will leave you one day. His body will die, he can't help this. It has to happen.

That's what I know with my head, but the feelings in my body are so strong.

The feelings in your body are strong. But to someone who is interested in Truth, it doesn't matter. Let them come!

Then it's difficult to come to Truth. How to do that?

No *how* to it. It just comes out of your love affair with Truth and your willingness to be really honest with yourself. Really look, "What am I wanting here? What's actually going on?" These feelings are there and you've had those feelings before. You know them.

Ultimately, at some point, you have to look and see what's your main interest? At some point everybody has to come to Truth. At the moment you have some interest, but your main interest is to keep your marriage together. That's just what's first for you. You just have to be honest with it. You can't really make a bargain with

Truth, "I'm kind of interested in You, but this marriage has to work out first." It can't be like that, it won't work. There will be some benefit, just by being interested in It but It can't kiss you completely, because still you have another interest.

I think that for Truth it might be better to be alone, than to be in a relationship.

This is just your mind spinning out now. You don't have to change anything. You just have to see clearly that nothing can make you happy - no relationship, no amount of money, no situation. As long as you think something is making you happy, then you're going to try to protect it and hold on to it. You call this love, but it's not really love. It's some need. So, no trouble, if that's what's going on that's what's happening.

At this moment I experience jealousy. I hate it. So I also experience irritation about myself, that I have this jealousy.

We can say *jealousy*, but what is the actual experience of jealousy? It is actually sensations in the body. Experience these sensations directly. What are the actual sensations?

It feels like a bursting in my heart and in my throat.

And then we translate this as jealousy, yes? So now, come to these sensations - no interpretation, no story, no trying to get rid of them. The story is what keeps us involved in the movie. Now remove the story for a moment and just actually meet the sensations, not trying to change them, no story and tell me what happens.

It starts disappearing. In my mind there is fear that it will be there again in a moment.

This is the mind tricking you. Immediately when you just experience it like this, the jealousy starts to disappear. If you tell yourself the story, "I'm jealous, because he is with some other girl," or something like this, that keeps it alive.

So instead of putting my attention to my story, I put it to my feeling?

I would say, not even to the feeling, which is an interpretation of the sensation, but to the sensation itself. Just let the sensation be there without trying to change it, without any story.

But if this story comes up in my mind, what do I do?

You've told yourself the story a few times by now. Did the story ever bring you happiness?

No.

So you recognise that it doesn't bring happiness. What drives the story is the feeling, the sensation. The sensation is not comfortable and you want to get rid of it. When you try to get rid of it and it doesn't go, then the mind starts to run. That's why I say if you meet it, it disappears by itself. Otherwise what happens is, the mind runs to the story again. It goes to the story and picks it up. Then the feeling comes and you start to spin on it again, and some idea, that if you spin on it, maybe you'll figure it out eventually. But it never works. So at some point you see the loop. Usually, there's also some pay-off with it. We think we get something from it. I can just tell you from my own experience that when I have been involved in something like this, there was always some way that I thought that it would serve me. I actually enjoyed it in some way.

I can't figure out what it is yet.

You don't even have to figure out. It will show itself. You just simply keep quiet, everything will become clear. You can't figure it out, really. The more you try to figure out, the more you get involved in it. Right now, in this instant, is there any trouble?

A little bit.

So what do you call *a little bit*? The sensations are still there? So now, meet these sensations. Absolutely go to the center of these sensations, fully. These sensations, can you bear them? Any trouble with these sensations themselves?

I prefer that they are not there, but I can bear them.

So you just bear them now and what happens?

It looks like it softens.

It softens. So this is the fire. This is a big fire. You just bear everything. Not moving.

I suppose I'm going to make a big mistake. I promised my mind to talk to you today. The first time I came here, there was this interesting fight with my mind.

I don't recommend to fight with the mind.

I can live with it like it is, it is not really heavy. My mind wants to ask about when mind is needed and when not.

There is no such thing as a mind. It is simply an ability that we have. Like this ability to do this with my fingers (moves his finger). If this ability is not being used, the ability is still there latent. It can be used at any time. Same thing with thinking; when thinking is needed, thinking can happen. Some thinking is very useful. If I want to go from here to the station, I need to think what tram to take. This is a working mind. There is no trouble with the working mind. Then mind is the servant. However, for most people the mind is running most of the day and most of their life, from birth to death. The mind is running and people are running after it, thought after thought after thought. At some point you realize that this thinking and thinking and thinking doesn't bring peace. It doesn't bring a feeling of ease, in fact it brings the opposite.

You are invited to see from where these thoughts are coming. Find the Source from where these thoughts come or find out who you are, or keep quiet, whatever pointing works for you. For one instant keep quiet and experience, "When I'm just quiet, there is no trouble." So simple.

People get this idea that they have to fight the mind or stop the mind, or do something about it. But this doesn't work very well because to fight the mind actually strengthens it. So the best is to simply keep quiet. Stay in that place that's always quiet - within your own Heart. Even when thoughts are coming, This that can see the thoughts is quiet. Stay Here, don't fight the mind. Don't try to change it. You are just interested in this Peace. Then thoughts can come and you see them; instead of picking them up, you just let them come and go.

So like this other girl said, "Oh, this feeling of jealousy comes." You see it. Normally, people are very involved and identified with it, "Oh, I'm very irritated." You can see this irritation in the system. It's just irritation. You remain quiet, you don't have to change this irritation. You don't have to do anything about it. You stay quiet. Then you can even act a little bit grumpy. It doesn't matter. It's not a problem. You know it's only a play, it's not real. The mind can function when it is needed, it's a very good servant.

Satsang in Amsterdam 1997

My Beloved Papaji,
what a divine mystery you are.

I cannot know you by name
Not Father
Not Master
Not even God

For these words are mind's folly only.

You await me where the mind cannot go.

KALI SHAPIRO

I see that I often put somebody on a pedestal. In a way I do that with you too. I feel ashamed that I have this pattern still. So the only way for me seems to be to close off.

Actually, this is not true that you are closed off, because you're speaking to me so purely and beautifully. You're coming and telling me, "Look, this is what my process is." There's nothing personal about it. It's a habit-pattern that you've had all your life, and you can't be blamed for this habit-pattern either. It's not yours. Somehow this pattern is there and in seeing it, you're seeing another one as well - this habit of being ashamed about certain things.

Usually we find ourselves in some activity that is happening. Then there's a judgement of that activity and a judgement of the judgement, so that these layers are created. You're speaking so clearly and so beautifully about all these things, of idolizing, of feeling embarrassed about it, ashamed of it. This means that you're already seeing it.

I see it, but it's not changing.

Don't try to change anything. If you try to change it, it means that now you're involving yourself in it. You're feeding it again. Just seeing it is enough. You walk into your room and it looks like a man is there and he is about to jump on you. You switch on the light and you see that it's your jacket, hanging over the lampshade.

You forgot about it. In seeing it, you already know it's not a man that's trying to jump on you. Just seeing is enough. You don't even have to take the coat off the lampshade. You see it for what it is. So now, this activity of putting someone on a pedestal, this is mind. It's only a thought. What did you say the second thought was? I forgot (laughter).

I feel ashamed, because that's also a judgement, that I should not have these habits anymore.

Judgement is only a thought. What do you have to do about thought?

Just let it be there, until it drops by itself.

That's all, simple. Okay, so now try on purpose to make me higher than you. Try to be ashamed at the same time. See if you can do it on purpose now.

I can't.

You can't. It's lovely. When people put someone on a pedestal, they project that this other person is involved in the hierarchy, that the other person is somehow wanting to be looked up to. Normally this is how we play. We find someone to play the other side of our drama.

Because I also project people below me sometimes.

Same thing, it's only thought. Somewhere you've picked this up, from your parents, your society. This is your evaluation. How you hook into it is the judgement and then wanting your behaviour to change. This is also thought - a thought about a thought about a thought. It's nothing real. It's like the barren woman's son. You can't kiss him (laughter). He doesn't exist.

That's true. When I do this, it's just holding me back from really sharing the love. And this is actually very painful.

Love gets covered over by these other activities, by these thoughts. You are not resting Here. As soon as you're trying to change, it means you're not Here. You're waiting for something later.

Is there a reason for the fear of sharing love?

People write books about that stuff. You look in your own experience. Don't believe anybody. Don't believe any book. Just Here now, no reason, no trying to change anything. Who are you? What's your very nature? What's your very essence?

Who can tell?

You are Love itself and you can't hide it from me. I can see it. Beautiful.

I have a great difficulty with comparison and judgement.

At this moment?

Yes, it's sitting inside. I feel it as a feeling.

At this moment?

The feeling is there, yes.

At this moment is there comparison?

Well, sensation of discomfort is there.

So discomfort is there. Okay. Where?

Here in the heart.

Okay, so this feeling of discomfort is here. Awareness is also here? Can you speak about Awareness?

Oh, I see that this hurts me very much.

This is not Awareness that you are speaking of. You are speaking of something else. We can come back to this. First we speak about Awareness itself. Awareness is here, right? So this Awareness, let's speak about this Awareness itself, any trouble?

No.

Let's look at what the trouble is. So now we're leaving *no trouble* to go and find trouble. Now, what's the trouble?

The trouble is that I'm judging and comparing my partner.

So this is the trouble? Then don't judge and compare.

I try not to, it doesn't work.

He likes to be judged and compared?

I don't know. We tried to talk about it, but that doesn't work either.

You find yourself judging him and comparing him? Tell him right now, "Judging and comparing is happening. I can see it's just the mind, that it's just an old habit. My mother taught me and other people taught me."

(Another woman): It's always the mother, why not the father? (laughter)

I don't know (laughter)!

That's what I thought (laughter)!

Actually, I'm making a joke. It doesn't matter. You can say the mother taught her, but someone taught the mother, and someone taught the mother's mother. Where it comes from, nobody really knows. It's nobody's responsibility, it's just something that got passed on, from fathers and mothers, from everywhere.

I don't agree.

You don't agree?

I think it must be convenient for some people, if it has such an old history, to say it were the mothers who taught us all those horrible things.

Well, what gets passed on, generation to generation with the best intention, is all the conditioning that was put on our head. This ability to compare and judge has been useful for mankind to develop from monkeys. We came from monkeys and by exercising this ability, we became technologically quite advanced. So now we are very advanced monkeys. But while this ability has brought us many things that we value, we've never looked closely at what it does to us.

It's an activity that has been highly valued and never examined. So everybody passes on, "You need to compare, judge and think." And it's not just the mothers. It's the fathers, it's everyone. It's the whole society, it's the church. Everybody is doing it and nobody is happy. It's not working for anybody. So when I said "the mothers" I was being very loose just making a joke. I see that you got the joke and didn't like it. Okay, it doesn't matter. You start to notice that this habit is coming up, right?

Absolutely.

(To the first woman): For most people this habit to judge is ongoing. It's happening almost all the time. Every single person we meet, not one of them is good enough. If you look at the way your mind functions, there's nobody that's quite okay. Everybody you meet, not just your husband, is judged. We feel separate and alienated from everybody while this activity goes on. We have been taught this way and continue it. The trouble is that we believe it; we are identified with it. We keep making these relationships that actually don't exist. It's just made up. Just like a set of reference points that are taken for granted and never examined. So you know, this judging and comparing is going on. Good, so you go to your husband and say, "Look, today judging and comparing is going on."

That means that you see it. You're not trying to change it. You're not trying to get rid of it. You just simply see it for what it is. Then, "What can I do? Oh, the mind is judging." Just a joke, really.

Thank you.

Yes, so am I forgiven by the mothers of the world now? Is this your mother? (to the other woman)

This is not my mother.

Oh, but you have daughters?

I have daughters and sons, the same number of both.

Aha. You passed the conditioning on equally to both? (laughter)

Well, only my sons have children so far and to my great pleasure, they seem to have got rid of quite a lot of the conditioning. And that's the best thing I can see.

Yes, that's very lovely. So, are you here also for the same thing?

For getting rid of the conditioning? Oh yes, I've spend nearly seventy years of my life on that and I will continue until the end, I'm afraid.

Let's look at this conditioning of *mother*. Because really every name, every label, is another conditioning.

Thought especially and they get labelled, yes.

This is all the garbage of the mind. We agree, there is no problem.

I agree with the way you explained it. Thank you.

I want to make clear what I meant when I said that you pass it on, because many people feel guilty about what happened to their children. Everybody loves their children. We all want to do the best for them. Nobody wakes up in the morning and says, "Today, I'm really going to mess up my children. Just watch what I'm going to do to them today." (laughter) Nobody does it like that. So it's not a conscious act. How it happens, is really through ignorance.

It happens just the same.

It happens just the same. That's why, at some point, you start to see that to wake up isn't just for you. It's for everybody. To wake up is the biggest gift for all of existence, for everybody. People say that you have been selfish to try to wake up, but it is exactly the opposite. To wake up means that you're giving the gift of being free to all of existence. Then you don't pass on the story to anybody. Everybody that meets you will be kissed by It.

**Like rolling stones in a landslide,
That's how we are.
That's how much control we have of this life.
Yet we pride ourselves,
on how fast we fall,
How much higher than the others we bounce,
How much energy we have,
How alive we are,
How independent we are.
Never once looking back,
to the gentle hand
That originally moved us.**

MIKE FLATT

In the spot where I feel completely abandoned, I'm not in touch with God. It's awful and it feels like I've lost it, and I can't get it back.

This is a feeling that you have? How do you know that abandonment is what you're feeling?

It feels so incredibly lonely.

You have to look and see what is *lonely*. Sit here now and don't move the mind. For a moment don't have a story. Now, tell me what you feel in this moment.

Peace.

Peace, yes. So what is this *lonely?* You know the lonely story?

I'm hooked on it.

Here! Don't move the mind. No thought. So how does this lonely story start? Once upon a time there was...

... a girl, she was abandoned by everybody.

She was left by everybody. Very sad story.

Even God left her.

Everybody left her, yes.

And nobody took care of her.

Nobody took care of her. So sad (laughter).

She can't do it on her own. She can't look after herself.

This is the story. It's a good story. If you're going to pick up a story, this is not a bad one (laughter)!

How come I get into discomfort when I'm in the story? I panic.

Well, that's part of the script (laughter). It's part of that story. You like it. You haven't told yourself the truth about that part. Have you noticed that yet? Look and see which part of the story you like.

That I get attention.

What actually gets attention is the story. You don't end up giving attention to *You*. Everybody wants attention. So what about giving attention to You? Stories don't need attention. Now you recognise that what you've been wanting is attention. One thing is for sure, you can give your Self attention. You don't know what other people will do, whether they will give it to you or not. So stay with this feeling of "I" and see what happens. Before the end of the evening I want to know what you have discovered.

•••

Normally when I leave Satsang, already on the bike my quietness starts to fade away, and when I'm at home all the bad things have taken over. Yesterday it didn't happen. I was quiet on the bike and I was quiet in my home. I put on all the candles and stayed quiet. I went to sleep and didn't even feel lonely.

Same bicycle, same home, you see (laughter).

I feel very happy with it. It's like what you're saying all the time, "It just happens by itself." When I was here I thought, "Ah, I'll never reach it and I don't know how to do it." And it just happened.

Yes, good thing.

This is what I wanted to share. But at the same time I have another question. I hear you saying all the time, and I have experienced it now, "Things happen by themselves. Don't give attention to your mind and don't struggle, because then your experience gets worse." But how can I get rid of an addiction or an obsession?

Get another one (laughter).

To change it for an addiction for peace?

Yes, an addiction for Peace. Get this addiction!

In the break I felt so alone and I'm so ashamed to feel alone here. It's so unwanted. Every time I wanted to go up to somebody to hug, he was already hugging someone else. I feel ashamed to feel like this here. Ashamed that I cannot take care of myself.

What can you do?

That's what I'm asking.

Nothing. You can't do anything.

I wished that I could just be aware and let it drop but it didn't work.

That's not true, you don't wish that.

Why not? Why do you say that?

Why? Because You *are* aware.

But if I would be aware, then I would not feel it that way.

Not *if*, you *are* aware. There's Awareness here now, right?

So why does it keep hurting me all the time? (starts to cry)

Isn't this lovely now, the crying and everything?

Yes, but before it was not.

Just remember that you're acting. You're acting sad, lonely, and embarrassed. Did you get an Oscar? (laughter) If you forget you are acting, then there is trouble. But when you know you are acting it's very good. Now you are advertising with this lovely voice here. Some boy will fix this, you'll see (laughter).

That's not what it is about. I just want to get rid of it on my own.

No, you weren't quiet. Men love to help. (laughter)

Still it is not what it is about.

There are many men that like to hug at the break. (laughter)

I just don't want to feel this way. I don't want the hole to be there, the wound.

The problem is not real. Where is this hole? Where is it?

It is a feeling that comes up and it comes up all the time.

So it comes and then it goes.

Yes, but it keeps on coming up all the time.

And it keeps on going all the time. (laughter)

But when it's there, it's so hard to not believe in it.

And when it's gone, it's very hard to believe in it. I must be clear, you don't want to hug on the break? (laughter)

I don't know.

When you know we can make a list. (laughter)

Isaac, in the middle of this loneliness that she is speaking about, there must be the same thing that is in every sensation, isn't it?

Of course. But you want to help her.

Well, maybe. I don't know whether she picks it up.

You would like to help her. But, this reinforces her idea that she needs help. It's no help at all!

In the middle of everything there is the same Emptiness.

Of course, it cannot be otherwise.

And, whenever the mind comes in, it starts to build structures, but in the middle it's always the same.

Always.

When the mind comes in, all these buildings are created. Right?

Therefore, no mind, no trouble and no mind means not to try to stop the mind. Simply, stay with That which is aware of the mind. Do you know the ten commandments? Moses went up the mountain and he came back with ten commandments.The first one is?

Don't kill? (laughter)

The first one is, "Don't have any other gods before me. Don't worship idols. Only worship me, the living God." This means that where we put our attention, that is what we are worshipping. Our attention is all that we have to give. So when you put it on thoughts ... thoughts are idols, they are concepts, they are not real. When you follow thoughts, then you suffer. Stay with the living God inside of you. It's the first commandment and if you don't get this one, then you have to abide by the rest of them. If you don't live by the rest of them, there's an eleventh commandment, "Thou shalt not be found out." (laughter)

So from this point of Awareness, from where I can see all this, I can see the mind and what the mind is creating and I realise that I can see this all in this Emptiness.

Yes, in every creation, in every instant.

Right, you can see it at once.

Even this *I am*-ness, even the sense of *I*. You can see it's empty, therefore no more trouble with *I*, no trouble with thoughts, no trouble with no thoughts, no trouble with anything. Everything comes from That. Just Silence, Peace.

• • •

This lady here, what have you found?

I can make the choice whether I want to give attention to something or bring it back to me.

It's not even a choice. When you see dogshit on the pavement, you don't think, "Should I step in it or not." (laughter) Do you think like this? No, automatically you don't step in it. It's not even a choice. Once you see it, you just don't step in it. Up till now you have been playing with the dogshit and the garbage of your mind.

It's a waste of time.

When you didn't see it, you were ignorant. Once you see it, you don't want to play with it anymore, because it stinks and it hurts. It's garbage. So, no choice even. Once you know, you know. And now keep quiet, and just enjoy. Everywhere you go this beauty will go and people will be attracted to this beauty. Just stay with It! You're not even concerned with people being attracted or not attracted. That's not your business. When you find This, everyone will want to kiss you and find out what This is. Someone who knows the secret is very beautiful to everybody. You just keep quiet.

In the quietness there is no separation.

There has never been separation. We've never been separate, not even for an instant. Like a wave on the ocean thinks, "I'm such a great, beautiful wave. Look at my lovely form." Even these bodies come from the earth and will return to the earth. They are an earth-wave, a seventy or eighty year earthwave.

**In that moment of absolute beauty,
It's not experience.
But simply that all the senses
are short circuited.
All doors flung open, so that
the light of God shines out
unobstructed.
Live in that instant,
and every moment is as fresh,
As a sea breeze.**

MIKE FLATT

IX

Is it necessary to have trust?

Somehow this urge for freedom comes. Then you go here and there to try and find someone who can point you to peace, to love and it's very difficult to know whom to trust in this. There are many teachers. Many people are saying that they've got the truth and they are very convincing. It sounds great when you look at the brochure. Many people trust because they want to find something. Ultimately it comes to a point where you meet someone who can point you at You, so you don't have to trust anybody. The best is to know for yourself, then nobody can fool you. You don't have to rely on anybody! When this happens and you recognise your own Self, then, by itself, everything is solved; there is no more trouble or any questions anymore. Then, when you read a book about Truth you see that it is speaking about your own experience. You're not reading it to get anything. You're just reading it, "Ah, they knew also!"

I think for most people, even during this process, the mind plays tricks. I know this certainly for myself. When I met Papaji, at first I was trying to figure out if he was as enlightened as Ramana. That occupied my mind for quite a while and also I was trying to evaluate what was going on. I'd say that's probably normal for most people. For a few rare people it's over - finished, one, two, three, just like that. But for most of us, we catch a glimpse and then have to walk through all the tricks of the mind.

So then we're in the trap again.

The beauty is that once you've had a glimpse, the tricks of the mind can't fool you so easily. They can fool you for some time, because we're so used to this evaluating, this trying to figure out and trying to make relationships. So we find ourselves doing this even with our teacher. But at some point it becomes obvious. At least when you come to Satsang, every once in a while the mind just stops. Everything is clear, everything is beautiful, there's no trouble. Then, again, the mind moves and it seems like there's something to figure out, or to do, or to get, whatever the story is. But ultimately, it's just this recognition of this peace that's here when there is no mind. It's starting to see this play that the mind does and just letting it drop away, not being interested in it.

This is what I found around Papaji. When you live in Lucknow*, you've got this whole community of people to relate to. If you think there is no drama in the community, you're very mistaken. Every drama gets played out. Especially the people that live in Papaji's house. It's very intense there. You really start to see every nuance of your own ego, your own arrogance, all those things. That's why people say, "I go home at night and it's more difficult." But I say that's a necessary part of this. Because you go home and you start to see where your mind catches and what it catches on.

The beauty of it is, that every moment when the mind moves – if you look – Awareness is here. It doesn't matter what's happening. As long as you have this knowledge, no thought can bite you so solidly anymore, because any moment, you can look, and see Awareness is here and this Awareness is pure beauty, pristine, untouched by anything. So if you're going to trust anything, trust *That.*

Trust is necessary to listen to the words and to experiment with what I'm saying. Because I speak from my own experience - not from what I have read or heard, the words have power and authority and they touch your heart. Then there's enough trust just to hear and to experiment with what I say, and something will happen. Something will reveal. It happens like that.

* *Lucknow* - City in Uttar Pradesh, India, where H.W.L. Poonja resided

There is a lot of trust. But the mind is doubting a lot, loosing this trust in you or in me.

So this trust has to be in your own Self. Don't even trust *me*. If you trust this body-mind, it will disappoint you because it will get old and it will rot and it is bound to have some trait that will not meet your standards.

What you say is right.

So what you have to trust is That which is the same in me as in you. That is what we're pointing at here. That you can trust, because That can never leave you. This is your own Self; this is the true trust. Anything else is mind only, doubt is doubt. You know the flavour of doubt? You know the smell of doubt? Yes. So you can see it. Like when you're walking down the sidewalk and you see some dogmess. You know the smell of it. To see it is enough. You don't have to walk in it. You don't even have to clean it up. You don't have to do anything. Same thing with doubt. Just to see is enough.

Somehow I enjoy very much being here. At the same time I'm not here. So as you talk and guide people in, I also go in and then I'm aware of the sensations. I'm aware of my thoughts. I'm aware of your voice. I'm aware of my body. I'm aware of sitting. And yet, there is a part of me that wants to be in touch with the part that is not here. I don't know how to explain it. So I'm not here and I'm here.

Very well described. Senses are registering, everything is functioning, and yet there is not a connection. It is just happening by itself and you are not here. Very lovely experience. Beautiful.

Can you point out who I am?

You know already. What is the doubt?

Thought.

Don't believe thoughts. It's funny, we trust our doubt; we don't trust the Truth in ourselves. We trust doubt. So silly. In the moment that thought comes, "Am I actually who I am? Is this it?" there is a feeling of dis-ease. Then we say, "Oh, this doubt must be true, because I don't feel good. I cannot be at home, because I don't feel good". So the thought spins itself. Right? When you start to think, "Well, now, what do I have to do?" see it is only thought, and don't pick it up. It's only a mirage.

~

Every time you speak about love, tears just come out of me.

Yes, a fountain!

Absolutely, it's a fountaining. Then my mind wants to interpret it. It's like I'm dissolving. My arrogance and all the bullshit from the separation, from not daring to love is going. This has plagued me for so long. Your love is just great. I love you. I love you very much.

This can't be helped.

I feel a bursting through inside.

Yes, beautiful. We're all so shy about love. We blush over it. Yes, I love you. And it's so crazy, cause it's not even "I love you" I love. I am Love!

The word grace is a little bit old fashioned. It is a very difficult word to grasp. As far as I discover now, grace is a deep relaxation, a deep trust.

Some people call this surrender. Grace has a lovely quality about it, because it feels like a kiss. Therefore people use this word. When they surrender, there's this kiss. You recognise it's always been here. The words don't matter.

Since I saw you for the first time, last Sunday, I saw myself gradually sinking into this silence. Yesterday it wasn't there and after some time, I started to feel uncomfortable. My mind went to the day before and I wanted to go back to that space.

What you're speaking is beautiful. Like this, the mechanisms of mind start to reveal themselves.

I started to label and then the greed came. I wanted to get there. Still there was a sense of seeing that too. And also a sense of, "This is it." But it didn't work. Because there still was some greed, still wanting to get something.

In one way you could say that you were efforting to get back, so it didn't work. In another way you could say that this efforting was revealed and exposed, so it was working perfectly. Usually with these things it's wanting to get rid of or change something that keeps them around. So I say it's working perfectly. At first, people come to Satsang and they experience a complete relief – so beautiful, so exquisite. Then they come and this stirring is happening – and it must happen – then again, "Wow! Of course! So simple!" And then again stirring. This is what must happen.

What was simple, seemed to be the most difficult thing to do. Because the first time it was just there.

It's always Here, you see, always Here. Many times I would say to Papaji, "Last night my dreams were crazy. I couldn't sleep the whole night. I was crying out to you. Can you help me please?" He said, *"What is here now?"* I replied, "Nothing." *"Good!"* I don't know how many times I've had that conversation, complaining about the stirring. And I tell you, Papaji is actually very fierce. He doesn't tell you, "Look, you can expect this." He just says, "Keep quiet! Don't waste your time on garbage, garbage is for pigs!" It also works that way.

I was trying too hard. When Satsang was over, it was there.

Two days ago, I was lying down, just doing nothing and keeping quiet. I could notice the movement of the mind. The question, "Who sees this?", appeared in my mind. At some point I arrived at Nothingness. It was very fresh and new and unexpected. Suddenly I could understand what you were saying, what you meant by being at the edge. Still perceiving, still the trees and the sky were here but at the same time there was nobody to see it . And for two days now, the mind really tries to terrify itself. There's a high intensity, very high, but there is peace behind.

This is a lovely report.

And I also want to say that I noticed that the mind is too terrified to speak of enlightenment.

Yes.

"

We take a break now. This is a break from formal Satsang but you can't take a break from Truth. Truth is always Here. But watch and see when I say *break* many people start already, "Oh, I can get up." Just watch, stay with You as you are standing up and as you have social interactions. This is where we usually go to sleep. Just stay with You as you are speaking with people; be with your Self instead of going into your normal social routine of looking for someone attractive to play with. (laughter) Just watch to see how this is functioning. You keep quiet. You don't need to speak to anybody. If speaking happens, great, no problem, nothing wrong with it. If someone is speaking to you and you don't want to speak back, that's also okay. You don't owe anybody anything. This time is for you, to be with your Self.

**With your everpresence
The sun shines
Through every nakedness
and vibrates all being.**

YUTI

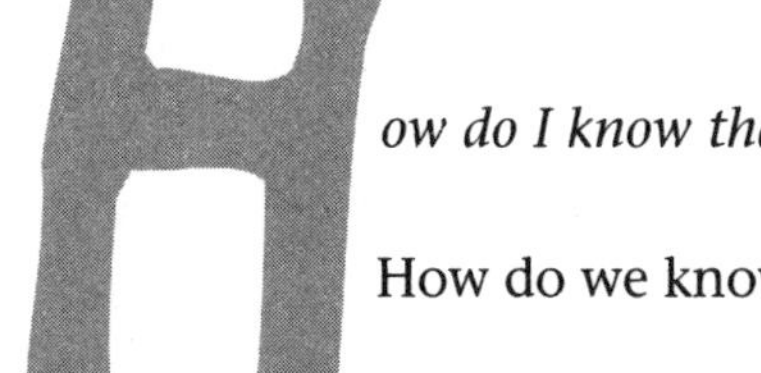

How do I know that I am this Awareness?

How do we know anything? It is a good question.

Can awareness not just be a function of the brain, a construct somehow?

Perception certainly is. There is a big debate going on now among scientists. They are trying to figure out what consciousness is. We start looking, "Who am I?" We look as logically as we can, "Am I this body? If I shave off my hair, am I still me? Yes, no problem. If I lose my eyes, am I still me? Yes, no problem. Arms? Yes, no problem. Legs? No problem."

Brain?

If I lose my brain there is no sense of *me* anymore. So, am I my brain?

If there is a feeling of I, *it must have something to do with the brain.*

Correct. So there is a feeling of *I*. Now we have to examine: is this feeling of *I* continuous? It is not continuous. In deep sleep we have no sense of *I*, then the feeling of *I* is gone. This is an interesting situation that we can say, "There was no feeling of *I*. No sense of time. No feeling of our senses." But what is it that knows this? Who remains to say this? Who is left over to say, "There was no feeling of *I* and there was no time?"

The mind notices that there was an absence.

But there was no mind, which means that there was no thinking. We can see our thoughts, and we can see that in between thoughts we are still here. Something is still here. In fact, during the gap between thoughts, there is no feeling of *I*. This feeling of *I* has to do with thought, with some activity. We have to look very, very carefully, because what I do know is that I am here. There is a sense of *I* here. *I* is interested in finding out who I am.

How do you know you are there, when there are no thoughts and feelings?

This you have to experience, and you can feel that something is looking now. Now this thing that is looking, what is it?

It is space, it is vastness, endless. No inside, no outside. But somehow I know that I know this. I can contact it, when I put my attention to it.

You say, "I can contact this." What is this *I*? Let's check this out. What is this *I* that can contact this?

It is the opposite of the I. Letting go of it, not doing anything, not making any effort.

But still there seems to be the habit to say, "I am contacting That." Actually, it is in the absence of *I* that you can experience That. So you can't say, "I am contacting That," because you say, "The absence of *I* is That." You said it very well. So let's examine this feeling of *I* now.

This feeling that is contacting Awareness?

It is not contacting Awareness, because in the direct experience of this Awareness the feeling of *I* is gone. So it can't contact, there is no connection.

I make a split. A thought about Awareness and then out of this thought I put my attention to Awareness.

Very good, very nice. And who are you?

I don't know.

Who is this *I* that doesn't know?

I am putting all my effort to get it.

So this effort produces an *I* that doesn't know. (laughter) This is only an activity. Now the activitylessness in which this activity is appearing. This is also here, right? Something can see this activity. So this now, that can see this activity. Can you speak about this?

It is light, bliss.

Very nice, now you see it for yourself. Now you can explore not doing anything. Don't make who you are dependent on stillness or no stillness. You're Here, whether the mind is busy or not busy. Whether I'm here or not here. *Who I am* is **This**. It's nothing about this form. This form is something else. Just a bag of flesh and bones, that's all. *Who I am* is in your Heart. Always. It can never leave you. Here's your own Heart. So This that can see movement and non-movement. Can you speak about this? People are always speaking about their experience. You hear what's happening. Nobody's speaking about This that is aware of every experience. Now you'll be the first one. You speak of it!

It's just enormous. I feel very touched. I am touched.

You are touched. What is needed Here? What do you need to let go of Here? It doesn't even enter your mind that you need to let go of anything. Everything can be the way it is, nothing has to change. Let everything be the way it is. So simple. We overlook it as soon as we start making any effort or any relationship with any experience.

I love the easiness, but without difficulty it seems like nothing spectacular is happening.

So don't hold on to easiness! Don't hold on to difficulty! Or do you want to become part of that cult?

Which cult?

The diffi-cult (laughter). Look, you're Here, regardless of any experience. It's a blessing when it's lovely, but don't go to sleep in that loveliness. Don't try and hold on to it. Don't make it mean anything. Then you'll recognise what's always been beyond any easiness, beyond anything.

I agree. I just said that with this ease actually nothing spectacular is happening. But I just had this knowledge that fear will appear again.

Let it come!

Yes. It wasn't, "Oh, there will be fear again, I still haven't got it." It wasn't that. And this is what I mean by this easiness. Probably it's not the right word.

Then you just have to take the next step and say, "I'm free. Easiness is appearing and I don't care. I'm free. I'm That in which every experience is appearing. I am That!"

I am That. *I just wanted to say it.* ***I am That!***

It has to be said. Even though nobody can say it, it has to be said. Nisargadatta said, "When I see I am nothing, this is wisdom and when I see I am everything this is love and between these two my life flows." So beautiful. Who can say this? Love speaking to Love. Christ said, "Peace, that passes all understanding." Now you know what he was speaking about. "I and my Father are one," not, "We will become one", we are already one. And that's why he said, "You can only come to That through Me," meaning, I am That. When you kiss it, when you love it, you can only be loving yourself and you're loving everything. We've never been different. We've only been That. We've only been watching the projections of the mind. That's all. Let this mind be there. Once you can see its tricks, it cannot fool you. A good magician can do some fantastic tricks, and you say, "Wow, do that again." Still you cannot see how he does it, "Wow, do that again." Then he shows you the trick. Then it's not even interesting anymore. You know how he did it. Like the tricks of the mind, when you see them, they cannot fool you anymore.

This woman here (points to a woman). Welcome. What is your experience? I've noticed, that you're sitting there, so beautiful and quiet.

Now I feel...

Not what you feel. The experience of You! Feelings come and go, this you can talk about in any workshop (laughter). What I'm interested in is the Truth of You. You're sitting very quietly here and something was kissing you.

Now I don't feel quiet.

Feelings are here. These feelings are in something. Something is aware of the feelings, right?

Actually, my heart is beating.

The heart is beating fast. Clearly. It's an unusual situation to be speaking in front of many people, especially when you didn't think you wanted to do this. So it doesn't matter. Awareness is here, whether the heart is beating fast or not beating fast. Awareness is primary. This Awareness itself now, can you speak about it?

For me it is hard to speak, it has no words.

You can't speak. Nobody in thousands of years has been able to say what Awareness is. So now, just to see for yourself: when experience comes, if you associate with this experience you feel as if you're not quiet and there's a sense of dis-ease. This experience is temporary. It comes and goes. Therefore the Sages tell us not to associate with that which comes and goes. Stay with Awareness itself. Even when the heart is beating, no matter what experience is there, don't make a relationship with it. It will soon pass. You stay with the Truth of who you are. You are always Here. I had to speak to you, because I could see you could understand. But this is deeper than understanding. This is something else.

I sometimes feel that it's a lot.

This is the mind again, evaluating somehow. This is beyond every evaluation. Any evaluation is only the mind. Then you make a relationship, "It's a lot. It's a little. Is it correct?" some evaluation, some comparison, something. This is just the mind playing its game. Don't believe it.

About emotions, sometimes I feel that I want them because I need to have something. I'm afraid of this emptiness.

That's why I'm speaking with you. Explore this Emptiness. Be It, absolutely be It. Any fear now?

No.

What is this fear? Just some thought, "I can't bear this. What happened to me?" Something like this. If you're associating with this, you have trouble. Some force is moving everything, breathing this body, vibrating every atom in the universe. You are that force. Why worry, why trouble yourself with anything? It is already the case. You don't have to do anything for it. It is already that way.

I feel good now, but to feel good I have to come back to experience. That's very strange.

Beyond feeling good even. This is beyond the beyond. You can't hold on to anything, not to bliss, not to feeling good, not to anything. Don't land anywhere. Your experience is true. You have to come away from Here to feel good, and this is rebirth.

I notice thoughts coming and going. Sometimes they just fade away.

What you're speaking about now, is that there's some distance from the thoughts, which is lovely. Normally people are totally involved with their thoughts. Now some distance is here because you can watch the mind. This from where you are watching, nobody enjoys This. People still like to watch the thoughts. But This from where you are watching, This you explore now. Tell me, you take some moments and just explore This. What happens?

Nothing and it's beautiful.

Nothing happened. This is very lucky. Beauty.

Sitting here, I still have this experience of Self that's continuing on and on. But I realise that I forget, when I'm not in the presence of so many people sitting. When I sit and close my eyes, I suddenly realise that I am not and I am at the same time. That's quite amazing.

This forgetting is just a habit of attention. You start to notice it, once you have tasted this *I am not* and *I am*. It's very beautiful. We call seeing the Self an experience, but it is not an experience. It is Beingness. And it's not in memory, you can't remember it. It's not like an experience; an experience you can remember. This is direct. Once you taste it, a natural process starts to happen in which the tricks of the mind start to become evident. So this noticing you forgot is the first step of this natural process. This interest in That is bringing up, "Oh, I forgot." Otherwise it would not even occur to your mind you forgot. Do you follow? So now this process starts to happen. You start to notice and by itself It starts to pull you to Itself. Just stay with the Truth of your own being.

There is a natural burning off that happens. We have had many things that we thought were important to us, things that we made more important than peace, beauty, love. These are all unfulfilled desires, unfulfilled dreams. Most people come to Truth with the idea that they are interested in Truth, but they also want to live their life the way they had planned for so many years. They keep going with these ideas that they had. Until this is really seen, people hear the Truth, but they continue the same way that they were going. At some point it becomes so crystal clear that you cannot deny it anymore. Then you find yourself just Here. Your mind just doesn't move. So, I'm very happy with your report.

I'm fighting with the question "Who am I?".

Who's winning? (laughter)

I try to understand the question and I think it's helpful to say it. But I don't understand the question "Who am I?". I tried to understand it with my mind.

So now, the way to ask, "Who am I?" is you say "Who?". *Who* is finished, now *who* is gone. Then "am?". *Am* is finished, *am* is gone. Then "I?". Okay, *I* is finished, *I* is gone. Now what is left?

Nothing.

Beauty.

If you were by my side
you would seem so far away
. . . . I am so glad you are me!

Yuti

How can I combine this peace with my daily job?

One of the biggest misunderstandings or errors is that we keep thinking in terms of *I*. So we say, "I see. I breathe. I'm doing something." Right now, your hand just scratched your eyebrow. Who scratched your eyebrow? Did you think, I'm going to scratch my eyebrow now, or did your hand just scratch it?

It just happens.

But when someone asks you afterwards, "Who scratched your eyebrow?" "Oh, I did it." But really everything is just happening like this. We say, "I'm working." We don't see that this *I*, that we think is working, is just made up. It's not there, it's not real.

Who is doing my work then? (laughter)

This is a good question. The same that's seeing. Who's seeing? Take a moment and really find this. Who is seeing? Who is thinking? You tell me who this *I* is.

When you work, you have a thought that you have to materialise.

Where does the thought come from? You see, your hand moved while you were speaking. You didn't decide to do this movement.

Where does this movement come from? Who did this? Find it. The question in your mind, where does it come from? Did you think it, or did it just come up in your mind?

It just popped up.

From where? We keep saying *I*. We're so sure that this is *I*. Find this *I*. Don't waste another second. Every trouble is based on *I*. "I have this trouble." So we have to find this *I*. Then we can find where all this trouble is coming from. What is this *I*? Nobody has ever looked. This doing is just happening. Seeing is just happening. Thinking is just happening. Who is this *I*? Really, take a moment now. You say, "I breathe." Who's breathing? When you say *I*, what do you mean?

When you give it words, it's everything and it's nothing.

So, who's working?

Everything and nothing.

Everything and nothing, yes. You let this work. In the East they have a nice way of describing this. Take for instance an ocean, on this ocean waves are coming. When a wave is there, we say, "This is a wave." We forget that this wave is actually the ocean. If the wave is saying, "I wonder where the ocean is, how will I find the ocean?", it is behaving like human beings behave. We are this Everything and Nothing, and in this Everything and Nothing a body-mind stream appears. It comes from where? It appears as somebody's body and is born. From where does it appear? Nobody knows.

What's animating this body-mind? We call it life. We don't know what it is. *This* is breathing this body. *This* is seeing this body. *This* is making this body hungry. And the body-mind mechanism has this ability to say *I* and to think, which gives the feeling of *I*. *This* is life appearing in this body. Then we identify with this body-mind, we say *I* and we think we are this body-mind. We act as if we are this body-mind. This is like a wave saying, "Now I'm not the ocean anymore, I'm a wave! I'm moving across the ocean, how can I be ocean?"

So this feeling of *I* is only thought. Very explicitly, it is this ability that we have to compare, to judge, to value, to make distinctions, to project into the future and to run to the past. This produces some sense of *I*. As long as we're involved with any activity, there's some sense of *I*. "I'm working," there's some sense of *I*. So as long as this *I* is trying to do anything it just makes the *I* stronger.

This feeling of *I* is an activity. As long as there's any activity, any technique, any meditation, anything, it just strengthens this feeling of *I*. That's why anything *you* do, doesn't work. Now, something is aware of this activity. This is clear. This activity you can see. Something sees and everybody that experiences This says, "Oh, it is everything and nothing." That's what Buddha said 2,500 years ago. This is what every Sage from every tradition has said. This is so simple, but overlooked.

But do you say then "non-activity"? Because whenever you move your body it's an activity.

It's neither activity nor non-activity. Let the body move. Don't change anything. You are Here even during this activity, right? There is Awareness here during every activity. Nothing has to change. Truth is already Here. Life is already Here. That which is moving everything is already Here. The life that's animating this body is not different from the life that's animating any body.

You take one candle and from this candle you light a thousand other candles. The flame is the same. The light is the same. Call it Life, call it God, call it Consciousness, call it Atman, Brahman. It doesn't matter which name you give it. It is the space in which everything is appearing. There has to be Awareness for anything to be there.

•••

When I meet my desires by simply facing them in Awareness, when everything is okay, then how do I lead my daily life?

If you're married, you don't need to get out of the marriage. If you're in the house, you don't have to find another house. If you have a job, you just do the job.

But how do you get the job? And the house and the relationship?

It happens. How did you get into a relationship in the first place?

There was a desire, there was a falling in love.

But you can have a desire for relationship, and still relationship does not happen. It happens by itself in spite of your desires.

But I have to be in time for my job.

Last year there was a man here. His father had been a farmer, growing apples and he was a farmer, growing apples, a very good farmer. I went to his farm. All the trees were lovely, healthy trees. He loved his work, but the borders got opened to import other apples and then it cost him more to produce his apples than the price he gained from them in the market. He was watching his whole lifestyle, his farm, everything, disappear in front of his eyes. Every day he got up and went to his work. It was out of his control. This is the truth for all of us. One day you can have a job and the next day two jobs, the next day three jobs, the next day no job.

We think that we are controlling everything. We don't know what will happen. One day you can be a millionaire, the next day you wake up and the bank is knocking on the door, "Look, there is something that you've overlooked here." You can have a very successful business, it can be going great, and literally overnight it can be gone. It is out of your control.

We are born, and this body is composed of genetics. These genes you have no control of. You cannot control whether you'll be tall, short, have big ears, small ears or blue eyes. Even your personality is a combination of genes and conditioning. You see kids that are separated from their parents from birth, then they meet their parents when they are thirty or something like that and they have the same personality traits. Genes, you see.

The other factor is conditioning. You are born into some country and to some parents. You have no control over the conditioning you receive from your parents, your country and your church. So this is going on. You have no control of the circumstances in your life, the input that comes in. You have no control over your response, because this comes from your genes and your conditioning. So none of this you have any control of. But we think we're controlling everything, you see.

How did it happen that you are here?

I don't know.

There is a schedule from a year ago. And you are on time.

No, it changed because of circumstances beyond my control. We don't know anything. When we really realise this we can relax. You can do nothing. Your personality is your personality. It's the way it is. You can't do anything about it. People go to groups and they try to change. You tell me anyone whose personality has changed. They don't change. All that can happen is that you see that this process, of this personality and these responses that are going on, is automatic. It's not up to you. It's just the sense of *you* that you have.

How did the thought come into your mind, "I want to be free"? You have no control of this either. Why did it happen to you, and not to your brothers, and not to your neighbours? Where did it come from? It happened. So this life is living all of us. This is the ocean. We are waves on this ocean. We have the ability to feel like we're separate. There once was a wave, let's call him Harold, who looked for the ocean everywhere, but he couldn't find it. Too close, you see. Though he was the ocean, he felt separate. We highly value this ability to feel separately. That's what's happened. Now, you just disconnect. Disconnect means you don't do anything. You realise that you can't do anything about it. You let it happen.

Then the microphone is falling on the ground (the microphone he had in his hand fell down).

If it falls it falls. Something keeps breathing this body. Something still keeps the ability to see. This goes on by itself. When a thought needs to come in the mind, it comes in the mind. By itself it comes from nothing.

So nothing to do. That makes it very simple.

It is very simple. It's too simple for most people. Because our conditioning is very opposed to that. We keep thinking that there is something that we can do that will make us happy. This idea that we can do something makes us unhappy in the first place. As long as we're associating with this idea, there is trouble. When you give up, you really stop, let go, here in this instant, what's your experience? No effort. Just Here. No trying to get anywhere. You can even let the activity go on. You are behind this activity. Truth is already Here. You can't discover Truth in the future or in the past. You can only discover It this instant Now!

The habit to get it is very strong.

Let it be strong. You can see it. Let this habit be strong. So what? What does it mean?

I think I want something which is not reach-able.

That's the trouble. When this thought comes, you want something, then instantly there is an experience of lack. There is some fear, that maybe you won't get it. All these things come in the same instant as the thought. If you believe it and you don't succeed, you say, "What did I do wrong? Why has God left me now?"

But these things are so subtle.

Not subtle at all. If you look, you can see immediately. What is subtle is Awareness, This that is underneath. If you pick up any thought, which is louder than the Silence, then you can't hear the Silence. Normally when desire comes, there is this play of, "Will I get it? Won't I get it? Do I have a chance? Should I go for it? Is it okay to go for it?" We confuse ourselves, there is so much to think about. But if you just meet the energy of the desire, you can look and see what is driving this desire. Then the desire disappears. It's not real.

So this wanting is here. Even this wanting, let it be there. You can see what this wanting is - some idea only. You can see that you are not even this wanting. Let the wanting be there; why trouble yourself with wanting? Nothing has to change. Wanting is here. Good, let it come. Who are you? Not the idea of you, this comes and goes. The wanting comes and goes. You remain. What is it that can see the wanting? What's This? You see, you don't even have to change wanting. You don't have to change anything.

I have a question about the emotions that I'm dealing with at the moment.

At this moment? At this very moment?

Yes, at this moment.

At this precise moment?

At this very moment, actually not. No.

See, this is an opportunity to be totally innocent and fresh. Really, to make a discovery here. For me it was the most important discovery, the diamond. Now is a great opportunity to see who you are. Not to deal with problems that are of the past and thinking about the future. This moment you are Here.

How come the emotions are so strong sometimes?

Sometimes is some other time than now. Emotions have to do with wanting something. When you want something and you don't get it, you feel sad. If you want something and you think you might not get it, you feel fear. If you want something and it seems like somebody is stopping you from getting it, you feel anger. If you want something and it is not coming fast enough, you feel bored.

It is always related to wanting or not wanting. Wanting or not wanting is the same thing. When you don't want something, it means you want an absence of something. It is still wanting. This doesn't help you much. Now you understand this: if you want to end all the trouble, you have to see who you are.

I want something.

Yes, this is the final want. The final want is to come home. You have to understand the nature of wanting. Usually there is something that you want. And once you've got it, you feel happy because the wanting is not bothering you anymore. At that moment you don't want anything anymore, and you feel happy. Such a relief to get rid of the wanting. So every wanting is actually to not want. The wanting is for this feeling of not wanting anything. So now, in this instant, you put aside wanting anything.

It's very freeing.

You don't want anything. Then what's Here? You find the Source from where wanting arises. Wanting is thought only. Find the Source from where wanting comes, where any wanting comes from. See the Source where everything comes from. What do you find?

I feel blank at the moment, actually.

Right. You feel blank. You're not used to feeling blank. We are used to being asked questions. We are supposed to answer them and be seen as very smart. Otherwise the teacher won't like us. Blank in most cases is not accepted. Then you think you're stupid. That's where I'm pointing at. At this Blankness itself, you see. Nothing is there, just nothing, blank.

I feel more. I feel a lot of love, energy and light and warmth.

The mind is not functioning, right?

No.

So we say, "Blank." But it is not blank. So now, when emotions come, it means that somewhere the mind is busy wanting something, usually at this age it has to do with some boy. (laughter)

There goes my privacy! (laughter) *Yes, it was a boyfriend.*

Everybody knows these troubles. We get involved with somebody and then we think that this person is the source of love for us. We are not staying at home with Love itself, with the Source of love. So this is projected on somebody and you suffer for it. As soon as there's two, there's fear. There is trying to control. Then we suffer from this game. We don't like ourselves for doing it. We don't like what happens when we get involved in this game.

Therefore, you are invited simply to see who you are. Then, if there is some boy you like, you can enjoy. You just be Love itself. You stay at home in your own Heart and you're in love with something that can never leave you. The Source of love itself. Then you can enjoy this Love with a person. He will leave you. Everybody will leave you, even your own body will leave you. Everything must leave you. But now you know something that cannot leave you: your own Self. Then you can enjoy the play. This body is attracted to another body? Okay, no problem.

During the day, when I'm out on the streets, I have many thoughts that are sexual. I'm wondering, is that conditioning from my father? (laughter) Or what is it? Because it doesn't make me feel happy or at ease.

It is good that you are honest. A survey was done and it was discoverd that most men think about sex once every few seconds, especially when they are younger. It's part of this body's chemistry. We live in a culture where sex is used in advertising and we are given conflicting ideas about it. People are not clear on sex. Women are dressing in clothes and wearing perfume to attract men. When the men are attracted, women like it and don't like it. There's so much confusion. The men want sex until they get quiet and start to see that wanting is not that pleasant. I also used to think about sex very much. Until I noticed, like you are noticing now, that it was actually suffering. Then, by itself the wanting started to drop away.

I've been experiencing for some time an inner contentment. At the same time it gives me a feeling of disconnection with my environment, a feeling of isolation.

So some feeling of disconnection is there. Let's examine this. Where do you experience your environment?

In all the people around me.

Where do you experience them?

Anywhere.

No. Where? Where does the experience happen?

In my mind.

In your mind. Now, what's this disconnection? This experience is happening in *You*. Everything you experience, the entire universe is appearing in *You*. What's this disconnection?

The disconnection is there as soon as I see myself as a body.

Very good. There is some evaluation, some sensation, that you're evaluating, that's all. It is only a thought, not real, never has been real. You cannot disconnect from the universe. It's not possible.

But in practice it feels as if I'm disconnected from the people, from the bodies around me.

This means that you want a man. *Disconnected* means that you want somebody to hug you. You have to be very honest. Disconnected means, you want somebody to kiss you and hold you in the bed at night. When you have that, you don't feel disconnected. There are many lovely men here. (laughter)

**Do we be the ocean
of infinite knowing?**

**Or solidify one wave
and suffer?**

YUTI

I have a strong pain inside. It's not bearable.

Well, if it's not bearable, you're very lucky. You can not bear it any longer?

Sometimes I manage to forget.

But now, this moment. Can you bear it any longer?

I don't know. I am also listening to your advice.

Are you willing to try an experiment? This will only take one instant, one second of your time. Can I have this one second? For one second, see if there is something that is aware of this pain.

A moment ago you talked about it, but I didn't understand what you meant.

So now, whatever comes you are aware of it. Pain comes, thoughts come, something is aware of it. There is Awareness here now, right? When I speak, the ears hear and there has to be Awareness of that hearing. Correct?

Probably.

Not probably. Just look and see in your own experience. For there to be anything, there has to be Awareness. This is not probably, this is fact, right? You agree or disagree?

I'm not sure whether I understand.

When you say, you're not sure that you understand, there has to be awareness of this not-sureness. Are you aware of this not-sureness?

Yes, I'm also aware of feeling slightly ridiculous.

So there is awareness of this ridiculousness, of not understanding, of trying to understand; but what's common to all of it, is, this Awareness. Everybody knows what they're feeling and they know their relationship to their feelings. "This I can stand. This I can't stand. This I like. This I don't like. This I'm trying to get rid of. This I'm trying to hold on to." Everybody knows this. Nobody knows who's aware of all this activity. So now for one second, just one split second, I'm asking: this Awareness itself, can you speak about it?

Can I speak about it? No.

That's the first indication that you know what this Awareness is. Nobody can speak about it. Now this Awareness itself. You can only be It, right? So this Awareness itself, what's the experience of this Awareness? Is there any trouble? No. What happened to the trouble?

Trouble comes when I have to do things.

And what happened to the previous trouble? You looked for Awareness for one instant. What happened with the trouble?

The thought had to go. There can only be one thought at a time.

So now, stay with Awareness. We're still here for a few minutes. You just stay with this Awareness Now, Now, Now. Like this. You kiss It. You rest in It. You bathe in It. You be It and you speak to me again in 15 minutes. I want to hear from This. When the mind wants to run for a problem, then stay with Awareness. Only one thing, Awareness, Now.

Many times I feel sad and I don't know why. I feel so tired. I wonder how to deal with it. There is no special reason for it and I don't seem to have any influence over it.

This is most people's experience. They are unhappy and they don't know why. This is your habit. It happens, but you don't even see how it happens. Are you willing to make an experiment? Okay, so for an instant, you don't do anything. You tell me your experience and we go from there.

I am very nervous.

Nervous means the mind is already moving. If there is a sensation the mind goes to it. If I ask you if you can feel the microphone in your hand, you have to bring your mind to your hand. It goes very quick, but you have to move the mind. The same with the nervousness. So then I say don't do anything, don't move the mind, not even to sensation. Do you follow?

I follow, but it's difficult to practice.

It is difficult, the mind likes to move. It moves here and there. It's always running and jumping around. So somehow, maybe it can happen, maybe not. Who knows? You are here and something can see this mind moving around.

Something in me?

Yes. You can think about what you're going to do when you get home, and you can see this thought. I can ask you, "What did you do yesterday?" Then you can watch the mind starting to run to memory. Something can see this movement. If I ask you to become aware of your feet, you can bring your mind to the feet and something can see this movement of the mind to the feet. This something that can see this movement, this we never look at. It is very subtle. You know what I am speaking about?

About consciousness.

Is this your experience? Can you see it when the mind moves?

When pointed out like this, yes.

So this Consciousness itself, you just be It. Not trying to see what It is, because then you feel as if you are separate from It. Just be It. Any movement, you let it move but just see it move, stay with This. This feeling of Consciousness itself. What happens?

It is here for one second and then it is gone again.

What happens in this one second?

It is like I am not here.

Very good. So now you are aware of *not being here.* Now you can see it for yourself. What is This that is seeing yourself being here or not being here?

Consciousness.

Yes, when you are not here, when you disappear, then immediately, one second after, you reappear. Like in deep sleep, there is no sense of *I*. Then again, when you wake up, this *I* comes. So at this moment there is no experience of *I*. The next moment *I* appears again. So what is this *I*?

It feels like a feeling.

Feel this feeling of *I*. What is this feeling of *I*. It is most subtle. Trace it back, find the most subtle feeling of *I*.

I notice that I connect "I" with feeling bad.

Good, that you see this! Keep going, keep looking, to notice what this *I* is.

It feels like conditioning.

What can see this conditioning?

Something in me, but I don't know it.

So you can do nothing about this conditioning. It is past. You don't have anything to do with it. So, what is very fresh, Here, Now? No past, no conditioning. Not trying to get anywhere, not trying to change anything. Just here. Be That which can see the conditioning.

It is like something within me that vibrates.

What is the feeling of this?

Like a watcher.

So now, you take a little time with the watcher itself, not what you are watching.

Watcher is no sensations.

No sensations. No trouble?

No.

Just like that, finished with conditioning, you see?

It is very simple.

Isaac, in the beginning of this year I got into a crisis and I started taking the so-called happiness-pills. I still take them and I hardly cry anymore. Not even when I'm touched. I wonder, do these pills influence in some way my ability to be Here Now? Is there anything else that you can say about taking happiness-pills?

What are happiness-pills? (laughter)

They are called like this. They don't make you happy, they just make you less unhappy. It's true! But there have been big discussions about this medicine. It is a similar pill to Prozac. I don't know if you've heard about it.

Prozac is quite harmful to the body. I don't know about the pills you are taking.

They say they are better than Prozac.

I don't know your whole situation and I'm not a doctor so I can't tell you whether to take these pills or not. If they are not so good for your body, it is something to consider. In truth you don't have to do anything to realise yourself. You don't have to stop or change anything you are doing. Let's also look at what is called a crisis. For many people it starts to happen spontaneously that the boundaries disappear for them, but because they are not around a teacher and they don't know what it is, they get labelled that they are crazy. This can happen. Some people can have little problems. Something is out of balance and then they need to take some medication just to be balanced.

I don't know what your particular situation is. I do know that I've met many people who thought that they were going crazy. They had some kind of strong experience and they didn't know what it was, then we met and we spoke and they were very grateful because they started to recognise what was happening for them. Nobody tells you what is happening; if you try and speak to somebody, usually they think that you are crazy. When you tell people, "Look, we are all one, there are no boundaries, I'm not even here," they don't understand unless they know the Self. So you have to see for yourself. I know other people who were going to start with this Prozac and they came to Satsang instead. As far as I know they didn't take any Prozac and they are happy now and they thought that they were very depressed before.

Somebody in India gave me the name Yalad, which means cloud. Then later I found out that, if you turn the word yalad around, you get dalay and one of the meanings of dalay in Tibetan is ocean and I feel so restless and chaotic. Should I just accept it?

No, don't just accept it! (laughter) Find out who is feeling restless, who is aware of this restlessness.

It has been a long time already, that I've been trying to find out.

No, it only takes a second. It doesn't take a long time. So there is Awareness here, Awareness of sensations, of thinking. This Awareness, not of anything, but Awareness itself is not an object. In It everything appears. Any effort you are aware of, any activity you are aware of, but Awareness itself, how do you know this Awareness?

You can't know it through the senses, not through thinking. Correct? Not through any effort, still Awareness is here. So this Awareness, how do we know It? We cannot see It, we cannot sense It, but can you deny that there is Awareness here?

I cannot.

No, you cannot. So this Awareness is here. You know this for a fact, deep inside. Can you speak about that?

It is somewhere deep in here.

Even this, something is locating it here. What is it that is locating it here? Something more subtle. Still there is some effort in trying to sense it. Trying to know what it is. You can't know what it is, but you are still trying. You can see this activity. The habit is trying to say what it is, somehow trying to get it. But you can't get to Awareness itself. If you don't believe me, keep trying. Awareness is here, you can't do anything about it and you can't get to it. So now we have to return to this woman. (To the woman he spoke with before). What have you discovered so far?

I'm almost exploding. It's not so bad.

I can see that you're almost exploding. Who is aware of this?

Sri H.W.L. Poonja (Papaji) and Isaac,
on Isaac's birthday 10th November, 1995

Pain is Gods boning knife,
Sent to cut through the minds flesh.
It speaks of separation.
Forget what you think caused this pain.
It was not that.
God was calling.
Come home.
Come home.

MIKE FLATT

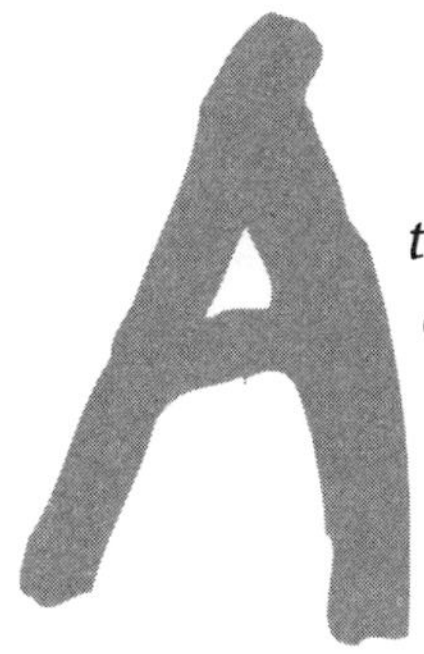

t the moment I have a hard time making a decision. I'm a medical doctor for more than one year and I want to do alternative healing or something completely different, but I feel decisionless and directionless. I don't know my goal or my purpose at this moment. I feel stuck and I don't know how to get out of it.

This is really a psychological problem and Satsang is an invitation to Truth. I'm not a psychologist and I don't know how to deal with any problems, actually because they all sound funny to me. I'm not a good person to ask about this kind of thing. I only know one thing really and that is Truth.

Tell me your truth about the situation in which I am in.

Forget about the situation. You're watching a bad movie on television, and you ask, "How do I watch something else?" Change the channel! You've been on the problem-channel and this is the Truth-channel. So, if you try to deal with problems, then your life is about problems. Right? If you're interested in Truth, then your life is about Truth. At the moment, you want to approach Truth so you can get rid of your problem. Many people say they are interested in Truth, but really what they're interested in, is getting rid of their problem. This is like if you meet a man and you say, "I just want to be with you, because I don't like this other guy. I don't really want to be with you, but at least when I'm with you, I can get rid of him." He'll be very excited about it! (laughter) That's how people come to Truth. And to find Truth is so simple, really so simple. Then you find the end of all your problems. Anyway, this just happens by itself.

~

I want to ask a question, but there's a lot of fear of exposure. It's a very intimate question. And yet somehow I feel that I want to ask you about it.

Please. Feel free. We're all in the same boat. I can assure you.

It's amazing. This very, very strong feeling of exposure comes first, before I even dare to speak it... I'm going to have an abortion tomorrow morning. And I have a very strong fear about going to the clinic, also about whether this is the right decision, the right thing to do. I just feel lots of fear. It's a very big decision to make. Somehow I feel a split. So a part of me, which is definitely the mind, very strongly has all rationalisations, why I cannot have this child and stuff like that. Another part of me feels it's totally wrong what I do. I also don't go there with a clear yes.

Many women have this feeling of, "Should I have the baby or not?" Even in circumstances where the man is there, he loves her, and they want to be together and they wanted the child before she got pregnant, this comes up. It happens for many, many women.

In a number of clinics that provide abortion, they have somebody to speak with you, so you can see for yourself if it's clear to do it or not. If you do it without a *yes* in your heart, you'll be torn. It's good that you speak. I don't know your circumstances and what is happening for you. As long as there is rationalising going on, it means somewhere you're not at peace with what you're doing. This you could see already. There is some fear coming up. This is prompting the mind to start to look for a solution, "Will I have an abortion or not?"

When a woman gets pregnant, often a fear comes, "Will I be a good mother? How will it be? Am I ready for this?" All this comes up. So any insecurity gets very strong and it's all on the woman's shoulders, because what can the man do? He says, "I love you. I want to have this baby and it's up to you." And the woman is experiencing these intense feelings. So you've come to the right place here, to Satsang. Instead of trying to solve this problem with the mind, which you can never do and that you've already had the good fortune to see – otherwise you wouldn't have spoken – you can take a moment now to experience directly.

Whatever sensation there is in the body, that you call fear, this fear has to do with the future, "What shall I do? Time is running out." This makes it very strong. This is mind running to the future and trying to deal with something. So now we have to put all of this aside for an instant. Just to see who you are. Okay? Because this situation is something that comes and goes. You're aware of this whole process that I'm speaking about. Right? So we have to come to Awareness itself. We have to leave the mental processes, leave the sensations, because clearly, You are Here regardless of any sensation. Many different experiences have been in your life and You have always been Here. Correct? So we have to see who You are. Let's look at this together. Who are you?

I feel something behind it. It's very little. Because the other thing is very big. But I can feel it.

Very nice. So what's the experience of that thing behind?

That this woman has always been here.

Does it even have a sex? You said woman. So I just have to check. Does it have a sex?

I can't think of that.

So, no sex even. What's the actual experience of That?

I feel I do get more quiet, when I make contact with That.

So you say, "I make contact with That." It's your own Self. So it's not that the *I* is making contact with That. All that happens now is you're returning the mind to its Source. You're not the mind. You're not making contact with That. You *are* That. But you've been focused on the mind. You follow? You said, "I make contact with That." **That** is who you are. What you are calling *I* is just the mind that is focused. So you're not the mind. This is only thinking. Your thinking now is coming back to its source. You are That!

We have this ability to focus our attention. We can think about things, we can move our mind from here to there. You can bring your mind to this *behind it,* you said. This is your attention and you can bring your mind to your hand or you can bring your mind to your problem. You can move this focusing around. You are That which is aware of this movement. This focusing is not you. It's just an ability that we have. When you focus on your hand, your experience is of your hand, but you are not that experience and you're not that focus. You are That which is aware of the experience, of the focus, of everything. Right? That which is behind. Now speak of this *behind*. What happens?

Now I don't know anymore. It's like I just look at you. I don't know. I can't find any words.

So now remove all the pressure of making a decision, of needing to make a decision, of this whole problem. Go directly to the sensation that's driving this whole thing. "I have to solve it. I have to have an abortion or no abortion. What should I do?" This is all the story about the sensation, that's happening in your body, right? So, we're moving this attention now. From That, which nobody can speak about, to a sensation which is driving the mind. You spoke of fear, but this is already a labelling. All that it is, is some sensation in the body.

Yes.

Very good, beautiful. So now remove the story and go right into the center of that sensation, not to get rid of it, not to change it, just to directly experience it. No story, no trying to change it. Not making any relationship. Tell me what you find. You already found it. What did you find? Tell me your experience.

When I close my eyes and I go in, it's basically a lot of things that are moving. A lot of energies moving inside of me. Around and around.

Now go to the very center of these energies. What do you find?

It's difficult. I feel different movements than before, but there are still movements. Still some movements in my belly. Some different ones. It's much easier than before. Before it was really heavy.

That was overwhelming and it was driving the mind and the more you thought about it, the more it upset you. So now, without engaging the mind you sit here. This appointment is tomorrow. You'll see, whether you go or not. Tomorrow, when you wake up, you don't know if you're going to go. You don't know if you're not going to go. You don't have to do anything. You'll see what happens by itself. Without any decision. You don't have to make a decision. Deciding will decide.

Somehow this feels very free. I can let it come the way it comes. I've been pushing myself for weeks and weeks. If I cannot go, I cannot go. I don't have to. When I cannot do it, I cannot do it.

Of course. You don't have to go and you don't have to not go.

Now it's like this. You're just Here. You've done every bit of thinking you can do about it. Okay, that could not be helped. It just came by itself. Hormonal changes, all these things are happening. You can't help it. Very good you came here. Now you just sit quietly.

If the mind wants to stir, you can say, "Look, I've played with you enough. It didn't bring me any peace. It just confuses me. So I'm not interested anymore." You wait and see. Tomorrow morning comes, either you'll find yourself on the way or you'll find yourself not on the way. Without thinking.

What a relief!

Everybody is breathing again now. (laughter) See, I was sure I didn't want another baby. One hundred percent sure. Then Kali got pregnant and then I was sure I wanted one! One moment you can feel one way, the next moment another. Our son, Arun is very beautiful. Kali was also scared. Because she never played with dolls and she never babysat, she thought, "I won't be a good mother." And boy, is she a beautiful mum! She's so beautiful. I can say, even *to be a mother,* is challenging. We're scared of passing on all the garbage so we're trying to be a good mum. When you remove the idea of being a mother, then this child will be very happy. You don't have to think about anything. You will be relieved. The child will be relieved. You just keep quiet.

Many people have been telling me about this. Last night one lady here, who was trying to be a good teacher, gave up this idea of trying to be a good teacher. She just kept quiet and now the kids love her. She is a substitute teacher, which is usually tough. The kids always try to test the substitute teachers and give her a hard time. Now she's having a wonderful time. The kids are loving her.

Isaac and family, Corfu, July 1996.
Top from left to right: Laxmi, Isaac, Kali;
middle: Rama, Arun; Bottom: Krishna

**When everything is served
on a gold platter
only a mind
could feel hungry**

YUTI

Usually I'm very willing to drop everything. But to drop my ego isn't simple and easy.

I have to stop you because you read somewhere "to drop the ego". Did you ever see an ego anywhere?

I think that my problem has to do with will.

No, no. First we're dealing with ego. Not will.

But ego has to do with will.

Where did you pick up *ego*? You read somewhere *"ego"*. Did you ever see an ego?

Well, it's difficult to see. It seems it's an idea.

Ah, it's an idea only.

It's a concept.

It's a concept. So to drop a concept, how do you drop a concept?

What you really have to drop...

My question is, *who*. *Who* has to drop?

The illusions about myself.

Who would drop it?

It's like to drop my defenses.

Before we can drop anything, we have to find out who is going to drop it.

That I don't know.

That's the trouble. You want to drop everything and you don't know who's dropping! (laughter)

I know it's confusing. I'm usually very confused. (laughter)

You've heard so much. So we have to leave all this. By leave it, I mean don't drop it.

I know somehow that I am already That. But the last years I've been trying very hard to progress.

Not the last years, now! (laughter) When you don't do anything, just simply here, fingersnap! This much time (snaps his fingers). What's your experience? Anything to drop?

No.

That must be a big relief for you.

How can I keep that going?

Like this (Isaac snaps his fingers quickly for seven, eight times). This, this, this... (Laughter)

No how. Too much *how* you have had already. Don't pick up another *how*. Don't pick up anything. No *how*. Too many *hows* have been put on your head already. Therefore, there is no how here. No how, no effort, no getting anywhere, no doing anything. Nobody ever told you *no how*. Everyone told you *how*. You picked up all these hows and now you're confused.

Molecules are vibrating the air, so there is vibration. Although you cannot see it, it still is there. You cannot see an ego, but it cannot be denied. It is there.

Wait. We trace it back, like you're doing now. We say a vibration is there. Who is seeing this vibration? There must be Awareness. Everything can only exist because of Awareness. You have to come back to the source. Awareness itself.

Could it be, that it is not awareness that you see, but consciousness.

Don't play with words. People are confused enough between Awareness and Consciousness. Something is seeing. Whatever word you want to name it. Call it Awareness, call it Consciousness, call it God. Call it what you like. Supreme Intelligence. There is Something in which everything is appearing. Call it Life. It doesn't matter what you call it. Something is activating the senses. Without it we say, "Dead body." Something is activating the senses. What this something is nobody can say, no doctor, no scientist. It doesn't matter what word we give to it.

What I don't like about this discussion, and I'm feeling it very clearly, is that it is going to be on an intellectual level and I know that This is not something intellectual.

This is a thought only. We are using the intellect to point at something. Now, if I'm pointing at the moon and you want to see the moon, you have to stop looking at my finger. You have to look where the finger is pointing. These words are pointing to somewhere. So the pointing is pointing, that's clear. The pointing can only point. That's all that words can do. That's why Ramana kept quiet. He said, "Words come from Silence. Therefore Silence must be much more powerful." But the truth is that most people are not ready for silence. There are some teachers, still today, who teach only in Silence. What happens is people get silent when they're around them even if these poeple don't have any background for what the silence is about.

So it is very useful to have an intellectual grasp of what we're speaking about here. Then the mind has a context to be quiet. Many people that come here tell me, that they don't listen to anything that gets said. They are not here for the words. They have heard the words many times. You only have to come to two Satsangs and you have heard everything I have to say.

You don't have to listen to the words. There is something else. There's an other invitation here that you can hear only with your Heart. I say *Heart* and again I am not speaking about this physical thing. I'm talking about, very simply, being with your own Being. And it's very strong. Many people come for the first time and afterwards the whole body is shaking. If you want to listen, if you want to busy your mind and argue like this, you'll miss everything. There's something so beautiful about being invited to Here, but you have to have the ears to hear it!

I think it's kind of unfair to disown the body-mind. I feel that it's all one. It's an intimate togetherness.

You have to make the body-mind a reference point to disown it. To disown it, is still some activity. I don't say to disown it, I don't say to own it either. Either one is the same thing. In between owning and disowning, what is there?

It's just Here. When I'm in my daily life, It's going its own way. And now with my walkman with the Satsang tapes, it all comes together. It's around, everything is there. Heaven and earth. It's a kind of "let it roll". So I carry along as it goes. It's fine.

~

I'm scared a lot of times that if I let go and everything flows, that indifference may come in.

Indifference is actually the highest state but people are scared of it. We're not scared of it in deep sleep. Everybody enjoys deep sleep. Everybody loves the state of indifference. Nobody says, "No, I don't want to sleep." Only if you're having nightmares, you don't like to sleep. Everybody likes to have a peaceful sleep. In fact, you can have every pleasure in the world, but at some point you ask for sleep instead of these pleasures. Then you say, "I have had enough of all these pleasures. I need to sleep now. These pleasures are no longer pleasurable. Now, let's sleep."

Aren't we on earth to make things manifest, to make this energy manifest, to shape?

Who is shaping things? Who is manifesting? Who is breathing this body? Who makes this body hungry, sleepy, who makes it think? What is the energy that moves the muscles? Find that Source and stay There. If you think it's you, find this *You*. Who is beating this heart? We say, "I'm doing this" and "I'm doing that." We never look to see where the energy comes from. This is our arrogance. We think we're separate, we are not. We know it Here, but we still act like the separation is true.

But when a thought takes over, what can I do?

No thought can take over. You take the thoughts into your heart, and you give them a place of honour. Then we say, "They took over." But really, we invited them. They cannot enter unless you have some interest in them, some association with them. Then you have trouble, because their nature is to make a mess, wherever they are.

There is a story of a teacher and his student. The student went to a procession of the king. His teacher dressed up in disguise as a beggar. He went to his student, "I am new here. Can you tell me what is happening?" The student said, "Everybody is here to see the king riding the elephant." "Sorry for being so stupid," replied the teacher, "But who is the king and who is the elephant?" The student thought, "I'll teach this stupid man a lesson." He jumped on his shoulders and said, "I am the king, because I am on top. You are the elephant who is below." He felt very intelligent. "I understand above and below and I can understand king and elephant," the teacher replied, "But can you tell me who is the *I* that is above and who is the *you* that's below?" At that moment the student's mind stopped. He fell at the feet of his teacher, "Only my teacher would go to this length, to show me my stupidity."

So beyond meeting, beyond two, where no meeting is possible, in this place you stay. This is beyond intimacy. This is One already.

In the whole structure of life, the principle of accident plays a role. I would like to hear how you see the idea of accident.

Like you say, it's just an idea. We develop language and in this language we have the ability, with our minds, to isolate and make up ideas. So we came up with the idea of accident. Accident is an idea that something that happened is unplanned. As if everything is planned! In that way you can say life is an accident! Every breath is an accident. But we don't speak like that. We speak of accident when something happens that seems to be out of our control. But everything *is* out of our control. So, accident is just an idea.

Ideas come and go. Don't build a house on the beach out of sand, for the tide is going to take it away. We've spent our lives running after thoughts and feelings. Nobody spends time with Truth.

I also wonder about the ego. Is the ego our false identity?

Again, it's just an idea. Nobody has ever seen an ego. It's just an idea that's made up, then it seems like it's something, but there is nothing there, really. It's just an activity of mind. Just some pattern that is identified with. If you simply keep quiet, it doesn't exist. The whole invitation here is to see what's real. So bring your mind to That which is eternal, out of time. *That* in which time appears, in which everything appears.

This is the highest quest. It's not casual, it's a love affair. It has to consume you. When it consumes you, there's nothing left. Only Truth. When your mind goes to what is ego, you will hover around this idea. Where your mind goes, that's where you go. So I invite you simply to bring your mind to Truth. Of course, you're free to do whatever you want. This is clear.

Sometimes Lord,
This dissolving in you is so sweet,
That the whole universe aches with it,
And runs melting to your feet.

MIKE FLATT

When I'm here, it's easy to do nothing and to reach the emptiness. When I'm at home, my mind is much more busy than here. Then I need your words, like "Do not evaluate" and "the gap between two thoughts". But when I need them, I am thinking.

This kind of thinking is very lovely. You are using the mind to end the mind. All these thoughts that are happening, are happening in you, in this Emptiness. When you have the idea to reach Emptiness, this is again picking up some kind of effort to get somewhere. The Emptiness is always Here, like the space is always here. Objects appear in the space; we just overlook the space. So if you try to reach the Emptiness, this trying to reach fills the space. Then you don't recognise the space. You are always Here. This you can check. Any minute you check, "Am I Here? Yes, I'm Here." I can say from my own experience that there's a natural process that starts to happen once you have tasted even one instant of This. At the Heart of everything is your own Self.

All of a sudden the thoughts that you didn't even notice, start to become very apparent. Somehow it feels like there are even more of them. This is a natural process; you can expect it. As you simply keep quiet and don't put anymore gasoline into these thoughts, they just run down, because there's nothing supplying the energy to keep them going. This is my experience, yours might be different. You're a researcher now. You have to see for yourself. Don't take my experience to mean anything. I can just share my experience. Many people say, "The thoughts seem to be even stronger now." It happened for me that way too, but now I can say that they've disappeared. They don't trouble me anymore. Different layers, different subtleties start to make you aware of what was underneath this gross level of activity. Then more subtle activities reveal themselves. Different attachments, different desires, that troubled you all your life start getting seen. And the pull to stay in this Beauty, at the Source of love, gets stronger and stronger because the mind isn't being pulled by these thoughts.

So at first, you really have to be determined as thoughts come. Our habit is to run with them. The whole of humanity is running downstream with all these thoughts. So now you've decided to go back to the Source where the thoughts come from. And this, in truth, only takes one instant, because this Source is always Here. You are always Here and this process of burning will just go on. There's a lot of ways that people rebirth around this process, like, "Only when this is burned away, then I'll be happy." But the Truth is instant by instant. Here Now, you are already free. You are Here, whether thoughts are here or not. You don't have to wait till these thoughts are gone. By themselves they disappear.

•••

I felt half empty and since a short while I feel half full. What's in the way of becoming fulfilled?

Nothing.

That's something.

Its only your own thinking, your own wanting, that seems to be in the way. So try for a moment. You don't think and you don't want anything. What happens?

I just feel happy!

~

It's incredible. I've been so busy with outside beauty my whole life. And all of a sudden I really realise that she is, I am, we are so beautiful! But you know, it has nothing to do with the outside. It is so beautiful, that I get goosepimples!

When you speak I also get them. This Beauty is always with us!

o

Isaac, during the last year and in the Satsangs, I find happiness and peace. For the last month I feel quietly content and I don't look for anything. I'm also content not to find the Truth and I'm content to just sit in my own thoughts. When you say, "You have to look for the beginning of the thought," I'm too lazy to do that. I just let it be.

What you are speaking is beauty. By itself; it's like this. You can say it's laziness, but once you stop, you stop. If you want to go from here to Lucknow, you buy a ticket. Okay, now your work is done, you had to buy this ticket. Then you get on the airplane and you don't have to do anything. If you run to the nose of the plane, you're not going to get to Lucknow any faster. You just take your seat and sit down and relax.

Now it's happening. It's like this when you come to Satsang. You don't have to do anything, your work is finished now. You're Here. You simply keep quiet. You don't have to do anything. This not doing anything is beauty itself. This resting, Here, is Love itself. That's all. By itself, everything else will happen. Who can say, "I'm content."? Nobody says, "I'm content." But the way you say it, sounds like contentment might be a problem.

One thinks one has to search for the Truth.

No, you don't have to do anything. It's possible also, when you're content, that you'll find yourself going along with various habit-patterns. But something is awakened, something knows. And, by itself, vigilance will appear. So you don't have to do anything. You just be content. Keep quiet. Kiss this contentment, enjoy it. Don't go to sleep in it. You stay awake in this contentment itself.

This emptiness that is in the middle of sensations that I discover over and over again, also in the middle of laughter, this emptiness - is it Truth itself?

Yes.

Is it true that this Truth is not interested in anything? Is it that kind of Truth?

Yes, yes.

This is what I've become aware of, while being here. I came here for other reasons. But the reason is not so very important, I guess.

Yes, it doesn't matter.

It's also very confusing, because I was really fed up with past-life karma. (laughter) You mentioned the garbage of the mind. I discover here, that you can't do anything with it, there is only the release. In a real way this is so.*

This is grace. You are That. You are the Truth of everything.

It dissolves by itself. Everything.

* *Karma* - Lit. 'action', 'rite', 'work'; the law of retributive action, the retributive moral force generated and accompanying all performance of action, held to bring back upon the doer good or evil according to the doer's motive, in this or a future life.

Everything. What you speak is Truth. This is the wisdom of the Sages.

I see now that all this past-life talk is bullshit.

Truth can only kiss you in this instant. Now, you stay with who You are. Stay right Here. So simple what you're speaking. Beautiful, from your own experience, no books, no nothing. You came for something else, past karma and now you speak very beautifully. This is Awakening!

Since once I knew,
it can never go again.
How can something I once knew
ever be forgotten?

Behind everything is
this unbearable silence,
big and huge
as the whole existence.

This is it.
There is nothing else
Things are passing,
they don't change this silence.

It always was
and will always be.
Nothing else exists.
In There is beauty, love, bliss and joy.

They are not it.
It is much vaster.
How can I really describe?

My mind is busy finding words,
and has joy with this game.
I can calm him down a bit,
like giving him a piece of chocolate.

No distinction, no boundaries.
All that is, is Now.

Stefanie

any things came to my screen, but now I can see I am the screen.

From here you speak. Let this be very fresh. From the center where every thought emanates. Any movement of mind is registered from Here.

I would say it's drunkenness and it doesn't leave me. It's total drunkenness.

Yes and you know the beauty? The bar is always open! (laughter)

It's always here and there's no cure for it.

Now you speak from this drunkenness. Let this divine drunkenness speak. This is what Kabir* did. He couldn't help himself. He would shout at the marketplace. This was flowing out of him. Other people are very quiet and shy. Papaji describes one man he met who was so drunk on This. He was dressed in filthy rags. He had an open wound and there were maggots living in the wound. Papaji said, "Can I clean this for you?" And he said, "No, no. Don't disturb them. They are eating." (laughter)

I'm afraid I can never shut up again. Then again, the addiction to Silence, I think, is bigger then the urge to speak.

Kabir - Saint, poet and mystic of Benares (1440-1518)

Silence will pull you and it will come. Normally, when people first find This, they want to tell everybody and they try. Some people see no value in This, so it feels like this Beauty gets soiled. You learn to speak only when someone is pulling it out of you. Otherwise you keep quiet. Then you recognise what Christ meant when he said, "Don't throw your pearls before swines." If you tell this Truth to someone who doesn't have an interest, it seems like you are on some weird trip, and then you may begin to doubt. So you just start to enjoy your own Self and people will find you unexpectedly and speak to you. You just keep quiet, that's enough.

Some days ago there was a lady here that had found something. Her friend criticised her, because she gave no attention to her problems anymore. That made me feel very nervous inside. I realised that I value the thoughts of my son. I was scared of getting his criticism and losing him. The day after, I realised that this being Here is very important to me. This goes much deeper than anything that I can give or get from my son. This is life itself.

You speak such beauty. This is life itself. The joke of it, and the beauty of it, is that in This something can blossom.

And my son is included in it.

Of course. It's only our fears that make it seem like there's some trouble somewhere. All of us have this ability to take any viewpoint. People take some viewpoint and that is normally the discussion, "I have this viewpoint, you have that viewpoint. Let's discuss it." And we could just as easily take the other viewpoint. But beyond every viewpoint, This nobody is interested in. Who is it that is taking the viewpoint? What are these viewpoints appearing in? In Satsang we look at this. What is Truth? What is love? What is beauty? Who are you? Very simple. We don't look at it as an intellectual thing. Just the direct experience of being That which you truly are. So beautiful what you speak.

I'm very glad too, because it gives me freedom.

Of course, total freedom. What a gift to your son. You speak like this and my whole being is happy. Everybody here, I'd say can relate.

I enjoy being with you, with the experience. It's divine and it feels wonderful. Yeah, it's the right place inside.

Very good.

Anything to say to me?

You look very good. This is the face of no face.

Recently I was with somebody who had just died. It was very quiet. Somehow the witness in me was examining it, was looking at it and trying to understand what was happening. I realised that the personality had gone and that what remained was very quiet. The form didn't contain anything anymore. It was just reduced to a form. There was a sense of eternity. What was there had always been there. I mean, you are never born and you never die. Nothing has happened basically. Somehow I have heard that many times and suddenly it made sense. I experienced it.

And you experience it even now. The mind creates this whole idea of linear time, and as long as we keep relating to it, it keeps us in this track of running backwards and forwards, between past and future. This is a strong habit but as soon as you start coming to

Now, all of a sudden something else happens. You touch something else. Now is not in time!

That's right. He showed me that. By not being there!

•••

When I experience something that seems near to that what you are pointing at, it sometimes seems so cold. It looks so unattached, so neutral that it seems cold. And you speak of beauty, I see love in your eyes. Somehow I don't make that step or I miss a link. Maybe I am still too much longing to feel warm, secure and loving.

This is not true. The habit of the mind is to evaluate everything. You say, "It feels neutral, it feels cold." The difficulty is that immediately when you're quiet, the mind wants to analyse this. "Do I like it? Don't I like it? How does it actually feel?" So make an experiment. Just Here, Now. Don't analyse it at all. Because as soon as you're analysing it, this throws you out of this Being into some relationship with Being.

But is love not having a relationship with it?

Love is. As soon as you analyse it, you are no longer Being. You are valuing the mind more than Being. If you want to mess up a relationship, analyse it! "How are we really doing?" People many times were doing great, until they asked that question. Just Here, when you don't think, just Here Now, beyond every thought, what is your experience? Speak from the experience itself, not whether you like it or not, just the direct experience. What is this experience?

Silence.

Any trouble?

No. But if you would ask me, "Any love?" I would also say, "No."

You describe it now. I'm not going to ask you to say anything. You describe it for yourself.

I don't know how to describe it without analysing it.

Just be it. Even if you analyse it. Analysing is okay now. You speak now, from here, your own experience of this Silence.

Vulnerable. But no safety. Now warmth is coming out of me that I associate with love.

A warmth that you associate with love. Very lovely. Keep going.

I don't know.

Just the Silence, you speak about it.

Unlimited. It goes deeper. No boundaries.

This is why it doesn't feel like the love you're used to. The love you're used to, is when there is love for another and this has boundaries. When there are two there is fear, when there are no boundaries, there is not two. This is a Love, not associated with passion and insecurity.

But what I mean is already not associated with passion.

This is something else. You just stay with it, let it reveal itself. This is enough. There is nothing lacking Here, no trouble Here. What do you feel in your heart?

When I try to describe that, I hear myself saying things that I have heard already so many times, like, "Now I feel it, but sometimes I don't."

So we can really only talk *now.*

So difficult. When you start using words, you have to start talking on a human level almost immediately.

Yes, we don't have a language for this. Good.

No doubts, no fear. Everything crystal clear. Still I want to keep coming to Satsang.

You know who you are at this point. It's clear. And now there's a love affair and there is a burning going on. You know also that to be in Satsang is very blessed and lucky. So this is the pull. I call it a pull rather than a want. Your heart is pulling. Ramana was drawn to the mountain, he was in love with the mountain. He had fallen in love with Truth. If you make it into a wanting, yes, then you'll get into trouble with it. If your heart pulls you and you find yourself wanting to be in Satsang, this is beautiful. No different than anything else, but let it be for Truth. It's pulling you now and that's it. Papaji, after being with Ramana and recognising himself, had certain obligations that he had to take care of. After his awakening he just wanted to be with Ramana as much as he could. He was in love. He would sit for hours, waiting to catch a glimpse of him.

Sri Bhagawan Ramana Maharshi

**There is nothing here other than a body.
No more than a tool
Through which runs a raging torrent.
Love is the sound of that river
racing in its bed.**

MIKE FLATT

You said that our behaviour just depends on our genes and the culture that we come from and that there is nothing to do about it, that it is just in our system. So, our whole structure is already made up then and everything you try to do about it, is only damaging.

It's good to understand the mechanics of Consciousness and attention. You are giving everything that you've got to give, to whereever your attention is right now. Just check it out for a second. See if there is anything else that you have to give. If I tell you, "Don't think of elephants" you have elephants in your mind. Whatever you are trying to change, means that's your reference point. So, trying to change doesn't work, just mechanistically.

I noticed. So when you had a perfect childhood and a perfect conditioning, then your life is easier as when you had a rough childhood. That's just there in your system. No matter how much therapy, no matter whatever you do.

You can say that it is easier, but it's not necessarily so. No matter what your conditioning is, it's possible to wake up from this nightmare. I have friends who are very happy that they had an unhappy childhood and neurotic parents, because it pushed them to wake up. They are thankful for it now. When things are going well, people are not interested in God. When things are not going well, they remember very quickly. Then they promise, "I'll be good." But that's not what this is about. This is about seeing who you are. To see who you are, it doesn't matter what the conditioning is.

And then the things that we feel will dissolve or just stay, or can you go beyond it? That is what I'm wondering.

This you can check even now. Your feeling has to do with where your mind is. As soon as you have a single thought, it is an experience, a reality. Like, if you think, "I want something," you experience a lack. You experience fear that you might not get it. If you get it, then you feel good about yourself and arrogant. If you don't get it, then you feel bad about yourself and the whole story. So, just from one thought all this is there. Usually people run after thoughts, from birth until death.

So we are Here Now. This is an invitation to directly experience who you are. No beliefs necessary. Truth has to be here already. You cannot experience it any other time than now. Not in the future and not in the past. Only this instant. Most people are very used to postponing. They say "Oh, I'll experience Truth after I've meditated for fifteen years." Always later. They're willing to wait to experience Truth but Truth can only be experienced in this instant. And to experience this instant means, that the intention has to finally come Home to its Source. People are running after objects, which come and go. Attention has to come to the subject. So you bring your mind Home. For the first time. This doesn't take time. What do you experience?

Right now? Pressure in my head. It's actually not so important.

This still means some sensation. Who is aware of the sensation? You. This Awareness itself is here. To bring the mind to Awareness is actually impossible, because there is not two, you and Awareness, there is only You. So this means that you have to **be** this Awareness. Normally we're splitting our mind, me and something. Instead of that, you find your own feeling of *me* now and you be it. Being itself. Not trying to experience anything. Not any relationship with anything. Relationship is two. This is beyond relationship. Just Here, the truth of you. Then you see what happens.

For many people this is very difficult, even though it is the simplest thing in the world, because you don't have to do anything. You don't have to still the mind at all, which means no effort. But people are so used to making efforts, that to make no effort is very difficult. We are used to struggling. We are used to doing and we are not used to simply being. Even an idea of being, "Oh, I'm here now," means we're still talking about our senses. But all of our senses are in the past. For example, what we see. If someone flashes a light, it takes one third of a second before you recognise that the light was on. So what you see is in the past. What you hear is in the past. The sages have been saying it for thousands of years. Now the scientists have confirmed it. They have computers and instruments to prove this. Whatever you see is in the past. All your senses are in the past. So now, we have to see. Actually, we cannot even say *see* because this is not seen, but experienced directly. So now, see who you are. This means nothing with the mind. *That* which *sees* the slightest movement of mind.

But isn't mind also part of you, part of consciousness?

This question is from the mind. Before you can ask this question, you have to take a moment to experience what I'm speaking of. Once you know the experience, then yes, you see mind comes from That. Everything comes from That, you see, only from That. It's not even a part. There are no parts.

Do we need to know hell before we reach paradise? Otherwise I don't know why Eve took the apple from the tree.

I heard another interpretation of this story. We were hunter-gatherers for millions of years. We lived in small bands, like a troop of monkeys. They move around and everything they need is there. They eat grasses, leaves, insects, everything is there for them. They really live in a Garden of Eden, a garden of plenty. We were living like this, then we found agriculture. So this discovery of agriculture was eating of the tree of knowledge and we had to earn our living by the sweat of our brow. Farming is hard work.

We weren't dependent on what we could find. Sometimes the animals have a hard time when there's a drought. When you're a hunter-gatherer, you are hunting and gathering and other things are hunting and gathering you. So we moved from this to farming communities. Then what happened next was Cane killed Abel – all the farmers killed the hunter-gatherers because we were in competition for the earth. People that stay in one place can build walls and defend themselves and have more food. They can grow more than they need. Many people live together, and they have time to make weapons. So the small bands were wiped out. Today, there's very few hunter-gatherers left, here and there, in the rainforest, and a few Aboriginies. In every society the hunter-gatherers have been wiped out.

This is our history. This finding of agriculture also coincides, some scientists and historians believe, with the ability that we have to think about thinking. A monkey can think "I poke a stick in this anthill, then I get ants." Animals can think, but they can't think about thinking. So as we moved into villages, there were different pressures. More memory was needed, to be able to function as a society. This ability to speak and have language also developed our thinking and our memory. So thinking about thinking started to happen and also writing. It gave us an advantage in this whole scenario. It made us stronger than an elephant, because we could shoot it. We were conquering nature. We were replacing our dependence on the gods. Before, we would pray to the gods for things. Now, we were taking control. We weren't valuing the gods anymore.

This thinking about thinking became very valued. And now we're all the children of it. This is the *I*-thought, which produces a sense of separation and fear. When you think about thinking, you can also lie. You can think one thing and say something else. Naturally this produces intense suffering. By itself, this suffering produces a wanting to come out of the suffering, and now many people are interested in waking up. We are the first wave of this wanting to wake up. Still a very small percentage. If you look in historical perspective. Buddha is only 2,500 years ago. Our whole history of this enlightenment is only maybe 10,000 years. A finger-snap in time. Today you can speak this and you couldn't speak it ten years ago. Nobody was ready for it. Now many people are hearing it. Somehow we are drawn to Satsang, to Truth. It's pulling us into itself.

"

Today, I find less intensity and less love vibration than yesterday. What makes yesterday's experience so different from today?

Memory, you see, memory. You have to remember what happened before and compare. Now, memory is an interesting thing. Have you ever told your lifestory more than once?

Yes.

But not exactly the same, right? Because each time you tell it, it changes. You see, the past isn't what it used to be (laughter). This is the same with all memory. Memory keeps changing, not even because of what happens afterwards. It is the nature of memory. There's an old married couple and he says, "It happened like this." She says, "No, no, it happened like that." Memory is very tricky. If we rely on this memory and we compare, then confusion is bound to happen. The memory is faulty, the comparing is also faulty, right?

About the feelings of doubt and intimidation, doubt is only thought, as is fear. In this instant, see if you can be afraid when you don't think. Just Here Now. What fear is there? Fear has to do with the future, with thought.

When I look there is awareness happening, awareness of many people looking and experiencing.

This is not Awareness, this is called perception. There is a difference between Awareness and perception. Perception is through the senses. So what you see, what you smell, all this is perception. Through the senses you get this information. Awareness is that which is aware of these senses. Awareness and perception are two different things.

When you have your eyes open and you're thinking of something, you can walk into a pole. The senses are there, but you are not aware of them. Also when you are eating a sandwich and you are thinking about something else, you don't even taste it. So in Satsang, when you are thinking of something else, you don't experience Satsang. Now, while we are speaking, you are thinking and you don't experience this moment. You only experience your thinking.

This brings us to Here. What is behind every thought, what is aware of every thought, of every sense? This is You, right? So you trust your mind, but you don't trust the Truth of your own being. You trust memory, but you don't trust right Now. You trust memory and comparison "Why is it different?" Instead of "What is the same?" You are the same, always Here. You were a little boy, then a teenager and now a young man. Have you changed in all this time? Your ideas and beliefs have changed. Your occupation might have changed. Your circumstances have changed. But have You changed?

I don't think so.

So something has not changed. Ideas, feelings, circumstances may have changed, but You didn't change. So, who are you?

I don't know what I am talking about, when I say I.

You can say that you don't know. Normally we are always looking at everything and trying to figure out where we stand. We don't know who *I* is. We are just looking to see what's going on, "Do I agree? Don't I agree?" We never stop this activity. So now you have come to this moment. For one moment just don't do anything. You just stop. Not trying to figure out, not trying to understand, not trying to get anywhere, not believing anything. Simply stop. Now you've stopped. What is your experience when you stop?

That I am present.

And in beeing present there are little gaps. Now you just wait, very quietly, and see if you can notice when there is a gap. You don't do anything, you are just here. Taking a rest. Not trying to get anywhere. Not even trying to notice what your experiences are. Not evaluating anything. Just here. What happens in your experience?

Nothing.

Just nothing. Any thoughts that are coming?

Yes.

Any gaps between the thoughts? In the gap, what is your experience?

Nothing.

So now this feeling of *me*. See if you can see what it is. Not happy, not sad. Just the feeling of *me* in which happiness comes, in which sadness comes.

It feels empty.

It feels empty, very nice. So in the heart of this emptiness, what do you find? Just in your own experience. You don't have to make up anything.

Fullness.

Fullness, good. What do you need here? Do you need anything?

No.

It is this simple. Any thoughts here now?

Yes, is there no question about who you are?

For me? No. Do you have a question?

What is really happening when I meet aggression?

So this question comes in your mind. This is a thought. As soon as the thought comes, fear comes and anger, sadness or aggression just from this thought. So you want to spend time with this thought. I am sure that you've spent enough time with it already but when you like some more, then you are in pain. Maybe you've had an experience with some aggression and now this thought is playing in the mind. As long as you are playing with this thought you have to face the consequences.

How does life look being empty?

This you have to try. Try it for an instant, one instant is enough. One instant in which you don't think. In between thoughts. What happens?

It's like I am not there, but I am aware.

And here you feel empty and full. Any trouble?

No.

No trouble. So now you just have to look and see. At this side there is trouble and on the other side there is no trouble. There is no problem with trouble; if you like trouble, you know where it is. If you like peace you know where it is. You can go where you like now. You are free to do whatever you want.

Stumbling Lord,
I landed in a pile at your feet.
I had wanted to lay my head gracefully there.
Lucky your feet were there to trip over.
I might be miles away by now.

MIKE FLATT

There's only one thing that's real. It is precious to me. To be here is something like being part of a brotherhood.

It's beyond brotherhood, it's your own Self. That's the truth of it. It's deeper than brother, deeper than father, deeper than anything. There's no way to describe this. No teacher, no student.

It's so familiar, it's closer than my mother. It's closer than anything.

This is the Truth. Your own heart speaking to itself.

It's like making love.

This is the mythology of Shiva and Shakti. In the heart, in your own heart. This is the true tantra. This is the Eternal making love with Itself. Your own Heart loving Itself. Everywhere, in everything, at every moment. This moment is beauty.

• • •

I'm very happy with all these people who know what to ask here.

Actually when somebody asks a question, they're not asking only for themselves. They ask for everybody. We're all in the same boat. There's only one Consciousness. Like an ocean, all these waves rise on the ocean. The wave is ocean itself. It has never been separate from

Shiva and Shakti - Two Hindu gods - the male and female aspects

the ocean. All of us are Life expressing itself. We've never been separate from Life ever, not even for one instant. When we relate through our senses and we think we're the body, we think we are separate, but this body could not exist for one instant without all the trees, all the oceans. Everything is one system. There has never been separation. Really give yourself this moment, to not seek anything, not trying to get anywhere, to really stop. No words, no understanding can add anything to you. For a moment, don't try to get anywhere. Find what's already Here. That to which nothing needs to be added.

I've heard people say they don't believe in instant enlightenment, but this is quicker than instant enlightenment. This is already. You see what has always been the case.

Teachers talk about having trouble with their students. When you don't have a teaching, you don't have any students and you don't have any trouble. That's why there is no teacher, no teaching, no student. Then everybody's happy.

I was looking at pictures of different masters today and the experience was kind of different. Are there stages of enlightenment?

Ocean is ocean. Sunshine on the ocean produces evaporation and the ocean becomes cloud. The wind blows and clouds become rain, rain becomes river, and river flows back into ocean. So when you look at it you see that now it is ocean, now it is clouds, now it's rain, now it is snow, now it is river. So it looks like many things, but it's ocean. The core is the same, always. You can have many candles: thin ones, fat ones, many colours, but the flame is always the same.

With one picture there was nothing happening, with another the whole picture started to dance, another one light seemed to come out.

These are tricks of your mind. Find out who is looking.

I would like to ask about the illusion of outer authority.

You are asking an outer authority? (laughter)

That's what I am asking. To whom do I address myself now?

Only Yourself.

Do I owe anything to you?

No.

This is enough. Thank you from the core of my heart.

This is freedom. There cannot be an outer and inner. Nothing, only your own Heart. Some people have an idea that a free person acts a certain way. This is a contradiction. A free person is free. They act any way.

I am here for the first time and I feel myself being welcomed in a pool of emotions and feelings. I feel very blessed to be in this presence of you and all the people here. And I'm wondering what we are going to do today. I hope we'll have some celebrations (laughter). *So when the mind is still and the emotions are calm and the body feels at ease, what are we going to do?*

To experience this, we first have to give up hope. And then no *I*. No hope, no *I*. Then, what's left?

What's left? Just sitting comfortably.

Even sitting comfortably is still some mind, some evaluation. So mind and *I* are the same thing. Mind is thought. In between thoughts there are gaps. In this gap now, you speak. No hope, no effort, no thought, don't stir a thought. No name, no form, naming and forming is mind. Now you speak.

There's not much left.

Very good. Anything lacking here, in this instant?

No, it's warm inside.

No lack. That's very unusual. Not even celebration is lacking. You have to find That which can never end. Never began, never ending. Every celebration will end.

It feels like a rock, this strength, this depth of everything. At the same time, it's so fragile and I want to protect it. That disturbs everything.

Yes, as soon as you want to do anything there is disturbance. You kiss It, it's enough.

I had a very strong belief that enlightenment is very difficult. That you have to sit for long hours in the hot sun and suffer. Now I feel that it's not so, that it's within reach.

It's closer than even within reach. Closer than your own breath. Your breath can be away, still This is Here. Anything that you get will be lost. Anything that you gain will bring fear, because you can lose it. So you have to find something that you cannot gain.

I'm spiritually conditioned. I have this idea that I have to do something.

Good to see this. For one instant, don't do anything. No effort, no time even. Faster than time. Now. This instant. Faster than this ability to compare. This which can see any movement of mind, speak about *This* now. Beyond understanding, beyond experience, what do you have to do for it?

Be.

Yes, it's enough.

To realise means actually to let go of the mind?

Yes, that's why understanding will not help.

I realise that, but just the thought of letting go the connection that I make, brings fear.

Fear is only an object. What's the subject?

The subject is Awareness.

So this Awareness itself. Where is It? What is It?

It's just everywhere, It's everything.

So now, what were you speaking of?

As soon as the mind goes back to fear, it feels contracted. Like this Awareness gets limited by it.

There's an urge to want to do something about it. When you start to do something about it, what happens?

More contraction.

This contraction makes you want to do more?

Let go or do something.

Trying to get back, or find the Guru, pray to God, something. Everything you do makes it worse; therefore I invite you not to do anything. Simply be at Home, be at Peace.

When you talk about it, you can bring me into this feeling of being at Home, of being at ease. From that place there is nothing to do.

I can't bring you There, that's the truth of it. I can just point. Then if it happens, it happens. If it doesn't, it doesn't. Nobody can bring you There, nobody can bring you out of There. Nobody can give It to you, nobody can take It away. Any teacher that wants something from you, is misleading you. I'm just simply here to point people at Truth. That's all. I'm not interested in discussions, in any ideas, in anything. Everything can be there. But it's not who you are. It's simply an expression of this body-mind. And you are not that.

But people can easily misunderstand this.

You have no idea what happens for anybody in Satsang. People sit here sometimes and it looks like, "Ah, they are really getting it." The next day they ask a stupid question... one second later... shining. Then people are sitting there, and it looks like they're really struggling and the next moment the most beautiful Truth is streaming out of their mouth, and it's not related to anything particular that I can see. It's not related to any answer that I give or anything like this. We're here and by itself this revealing starts to happen. Nobody's doing anything.

I know it in my own experience. I would sit in Satsang sometimes, being judgemental, bored, doubting, irritated at having to sit uncomfortably. Then somehow in the midst of all of that, the mind got quiet by itself. This love started to happen by itself. Love is just love. You just keep quiet and it shows itself. Like the sun shines everywhere. It doesn't care if somebody says, "Oh, I like it.", or, "It's too much." It just shines. That is its nature.

—

Every day I find out that all my questions are asked and answered. Sometimes it's like it drops inside and it becomes an alive experience. At the moment I feel inside like water is flowing through me.

I also have this experience.

It feels so clean. I can see that whatever you feel or give words to, is an experience that is seen in Awareness. I always thought that I had to search for things and at some point in life I stopped searching because I thought it had no use. It only brings you down. But after all I was still searching. I was flowing down this stream. Everything was going natural. I didn't care and the feeling is great. I know that I am just Here Now.

Ah, beautiful.

I don't have to do anything. Everything is one. Outside and inside. Good or bad. It's all perfect. So there's nothing to do and that's great. But the problem is... (laughter) *my family and friends. I call it my past life. They cannot follow and I'm losing them. I feel that I am losing them like all the habits.*

How lucky, yeah?

It's not like that. Most of the habits that I lost were not so good. But the people I lose, I love very much. I want to take them with me on this road. It hurts me very much. Not that I'm afraid to be alone, because I am not alone, you know.

Yes, it's clear. Now you have to make an experiment here. Be willing to lose them. What happens?

I just let go. I dreamt this already. That it just has to be like this. I cried a lot about it, but there's no point of return.

Your crying doesn't matter. The letting go is the only thing and then you'll see what will happen. When you try and pull a donkey, it goes backwards. When you don't do anything, see what happens.

It's all the same story, isn't it?

It's the same story. When you want to take someone with you, they say "no, no". When you actually let go completely, that pain of trying to pull will be gone. Anything can happen then. Somehow people are seeing for themselves what's there for them. I have a teenage daughter. Teenagers are in an interesting phase of growing up because they actually have to reject everything of their parents. This is natural, because this is how they come to have their own values. When you are a parent, it is natural to want to turn your kids on to what you find beautiful. So I wanted her very much to know about Satsang, and she didn't want to know. So I completely let go of wanting her to know. Then she still decided not to be in Satsang with me, but she fell in love with Papaji.

It doesn't make a difference.

It doesn't make a difference. Lovely to hear what you spoke and just to feel your openness. I could hear from the start that there was some trouble when you were speaking. Now this trouble is gone.

I felt unhappiness because of a man I loved. He is gone. I can see clearly now, that there is only love. There is no story.

Oh beautiful. You give up the love story and then you have Love.

Falling into the trap of thinking, of thoughts, what do you do?

Within moments it is noticed and I am not interested in it. Like tonight, I called a taxi to come here and there was a waiting list of twelve and when it got down to one, the phone was disconnected. When I called again, the phone was busy for ten minutes, and by then I should already be in Satsang. When I called again, I was number twelve in line. Once before I had called the taxi asking, "Can I call ahead of time?" And they said "No, you just call two minutes before." I was pissed off for being late. I noticed this feeling in my body and that my personality type is very blaming, I felt this urge to blame someone. But I could see it, realising there is nothing I could do, and then it passed, just like that.

Now I can see what Papaji meant saying "We are all enlightened."

It is very simple, the whole thing. It is amazing, things come up, and there is no urge to change them, they just come up and they go. It just happens. Like the weather, it has nothing to do with who I am.

Are there any last minute questions?

Who are you?

I am **That** in which the senses appear, through the senses the whole universe. I am **That** in which thoughts appear. Through thoughts the whole relationship with the universe and the ability to compare. I am **That** in which everything appears. Time, space, this entire universe. **I am That!**

Namaskar.

For more information
about Satsang with Isaac
and to receive a schedule contact:

Deva Stadler
Hutbergstr. 14 b, 85256 Pasenbach, Germany

or see the Internet
http://www.om.com.au/isaac

Isaac and Kali, Castle Plankenstein, Austria, 1997